THE ST. LOUIS
CARDINALS

BY DONALD HONIG

Nonfiction

Baseball When the Grass Was Real
Baseball Between the Lines
The Man in the Dugout
The October Heroes
The Image of Their Greatness (with Lawrence Ritter)
The 100 Greatest Baseball Players of All Time (with Lawrence Ritter)
The Brooklyn Dodgers: An Illustrated Tribute
The New York Yankees: An Illustrated History
Baseball's 10 Greatest Teams
The Los Angeles Dodgers: The First Quarter Century
The National League: An Illustrated History
The American League: An Illustrated History
Baseball America
The New York Mets: The First Quarter Century
The World Series: An Illustrated History
Baseball in the '50s
The All-Star Game: An Illustrated History
Mays, Mantle, Snider: A Celebration
The Greatest First Basemen of All Time
The Greatest Pitchers of All Time
A Donald Honig Reader
Baseball in the '30s
The Power Hitters
1959: The Year That Was
American League MVP's
National League Rookies of the Year
National League MVP's
American League Rookies of the Year
1961: The Year That Was
Baseball: An Illustrated History of America's Game
The Boston Red Sox: An Illustrated History

Fiction

Sidewalk Caesar
Walk Like a Man
The Americans
Divide the Night
No Song to Sing
Judgment Night
The Love Thief
The Severith Style
Illusions
I Should Have Sold Petunias
The Last Great Season
Marching Home

THE ST. LOUIS
CARDINALS

AN ILLUSTRATED HISTORY

◆

DONALD HONIG

PRENTICE
HALL
PRESS

New York London Toronto Sydney Tokyo Singapore

Prentice Hall Press
15 Columbus Circle
New York, New York 10023

PRENTICE HALL PRESS and colophons are registered trademarks of Simon & Schuster, Inc.

Library of Congress Cataloging-in-Publication Data

Honig, Donald.
    The St. Louis Cardinals: an illustrated history / Donald Honig.
      p. cm.
    Includes index.
    ISBN 0-13-840026-1
    1. St. Louis Cardinals (Baseball team)—History. I. Title.
  II. Title: Saint Louis Cardinals.
  GV875.S3H64 1991
  796.357′64′0977866—dc20   90-36331
                                              CIP

Designed by Robert Bull Design

Manufactured in the United States of America

10 9 8 7 6 5 4 3 2 1

First Edition

For My Daughter, Catherine

ACKNOWLEDGMENTS

I am deeply indebted to a number of people for their generous assistance in photo research and help in gathering the photographs reproduced in this book. Special thanks go to Michael P. Aronstein, president of TV Sports Mailbag, and his son Andrew, for their help; to Patricia Kelly and her colleagues at the National Baseball Hall of Fame and Museum at Cooperstown, New York; and Steve Gietschier of *The Sporting News.* The remaining photographs are from the following sources: p. 194 (bottom), Russ Reed; pps. 197 (left) and 202 (bottom), Nancy Hogue; p. 205 (right), Tim Parker; p. 210 (left), Nancy Hogue; pps. 223 and 226, Rich Pilling; p. 228 (right), Chuck Rydlewski; p. 229 (left), Michael Ponzini; p. 230 (left), Jeff Caplick; p. 230 (right), Rich Pilling; p. 234, Vic Milton.

For his constant encouragement and support, a heartfelt thanks to Kip Ingle, director of public and media relations for the St. Louis Cardinals.

Also, for their advice and counsel, a word of thanks to the following: Stanley Honig, Lawrence Ritter, David Markson, Douglas Mulcahy, Mary E. Gallagher, James Trudeau, and Thomas, James, and Michael Brookman.

And a final thank-you to my baseball-wise editor Paul Aron.

CONTENTS

INTRODUCTION

Several years ago, when a traveler from the East landed in St. Louis to conduct some business in the Midwest, he was greeted at the airport with a handshake and the salutation, "Welcome to Cardinal country."

A walk through the Busch Stadium parking area at game time gives graphic evidence of the expansive appeal of the St. Louis Cardinals; not only is the state of Missouri amply represented but one sees automobiles and chartered buses from Illinois, Iowa, Arkansas, Oklahoma, Kansas, and other regions of middle-America that form the far-flung wellsprings of Cardinal fervor.

The St. Louis Cardinals are the heart of baseball in the heartland of America. They are also one of the few teams that have transcended their own geography and attracted fans from around the country. Many American League fans who have no great interest in the National League but who feel they need a rooting interest to achieve season-long "balance" have adopted the Cardinals as their second team. The reasons are several. Some people have been drawn by the élan of the Cardinal style of play—pitching, defense, daring baserunning—which is seen by some as baseball at its purest, a style that the Cardinals have employed so consistently and for so long it has almost become a corporate image. Others simply became fascinated by one Cardinal star or another—Hornsby or Dean or Medwick or Musial or Brock—and stayed to root on and on. Some have been attracted by that classic uniform with its red piping and pair of crested cardinals poised on their resting bat.

"We watch 'em all summer and then talk about 'em all winter," one venerable Cardinal devotee has said. "And the talk goes back and back and back." For St. Louis fans, this is pleasurable talk, for their colorful and attractive team has won fifteen pennants and nine world championships, has had twenty batting champions and fourteen Most Valuable Players. And the feeling in Cardinal country is that the best is yet to come.

A SHAKY BEGINNING

UP UNTIL THE TIME THE Brooklyn Dodgers and New York Giants moved to the West Coast in 1957, the St. Louis Cardinals were baseball's frontier team, the only major league club west of the Mississippi. To some Easterners, this geographic fact made the men from St. Louis seem swaggering and slightly exotic, the embodiment of frontier characteristics—ruggedness, a quickness to improvise, daring, mastery of the unexpected. And there were certain Cardinal teams, particularly of "The Gashouse Gang" era and the early 1940s, that played right up to the edge of this image.

The basis of much Cardinal lore is the farm system designed and built by Branch Rickey. It began producing harvests of gifted young players in the 1920s, players who came to the major leagues with a spirit, pride, and unified approach to the game that had been drilled into them by Rickey and his associates.

Because of the talent that crowded the Cardinal farm system at its peak (and at its peak, in the 1930s, it had as many as fifty teams and eight hundred players), it was not uncommon for a player to serve a five- or six-year apprenticeship at outposts of the Cardinal empire (young Ted Williams spurned a Cardinal offer because "they had a huge farm system then and you could get lost"). So when a player finally did reach the big club it was after the most exacting winnowing process in baseball; he was a man hardened by years and years of minor league experience, he was weathered and well-traveled, he had truly earned a spot in the big leagues and he meant to keep it. Since most

of the Cardinal players were ingrained with this attitude, a recognizable team persona was shaped, its contours visible to this day.

St. Louis was a charter member when the National League was formed in 1876. Other members of the brand-new eight-team operation were Chicago, Cincinnati, Boston, New York, Philadelphia, Louisville, and Hartford. (Only Chicago has maintained a record of unbroken membership from the formation of the league to the present.) It was a historic year for the United States, as the country celebrated the 100th anniversary of the signing of the Declaration of Independence, delighted in the publication of Mark Twain's *Tom Sawyer,* and was stunned by the annihilation of General George Armstrong Custer and his command at the Little Bighorn.

Known as the Browns in those formative years, that first St. Louis club finished in second place, which, incredibly, was as high as a St. Louis National League club was to rise until taking its first pennant in 1926, exactly a half-century later. The club played just 64 games in that long-ago first season, ending with a fine 45–19 record, second to Chicago's 52–14 mark. A twenty-four-year-old right-hander named George Washington Bradley pitched every game for the team, which was not an uncommon feat at the time (four teams in the league employed just a single pitcher that year), and among his 45 wins was the league's first no-hitter, against Hartford on July 15.

Still struggling in embryo, the league shrank to six teams in 1877, with St. Louis finishing fourth. It was a freewheeling era in profes-

Chris Von Der Ahe, the first great character in St. Louis baseball history.

sional baseball, and in an effort to improve his club, team president John Lucas signed to St. Louis contracts five top players from the Louisville club, which had finished second. The addition of these players raised pennant expectations in St. Louis for 1878, but before the season opened it was determined that four of the Louisville stars had conspired to throw games the previous season. League president William Hulbert, who ran his operation with an iron hand and was determined to reassure the public about the integrity of his fledgling

game, permanently barred the offending foursome from professional baseball.

This sordid turn of events so soured John Lucas that he broke up his club and resigned from the league, temporarily ending St. Louis's membership in the major league fraternity.

Though teams continued to come and go over the next few years, the National League flourished as America's fascination with the new game intensified. Inevitably, the National League's monopoly was challenged. In 1882, another major league, calling itself the American Association, was formed. This new confection, which lasted until 1891, included a port of call in St. Louis.

The American Association's St. Louis club, also known as the Browns, was backed by one Chris Von Der Ahe, one of the city's most ostentatious characters. The German-born Von Der Ahe spoke with an accent that seemed to have wafted straight out of dishes of sauerbraten and scuttles of beer, referring to the game as "paseball" and himself as "bresident" of the club. Chris owned a beer garden not far from the Grand Avenue and Dodier Street site where the Browns played their games (the same site where the Cardinals' Sportsman's Park would rise).

The round-bellied Von Der Ahe wore stovepipe hats, gaudy waistcoats, diamond stickpins, and was known as a ladies' man. Something of a showman, Chris made a festive event of transporting his players from their hotel to the playing grounds, seating them in open carriages pulled by horses draped with St. Louis Browns blankets.

Von Der Ahe's baseball adviser was Al Spink, who with his brother founded *The Sporting News*. It was at Spink's suggestion that the Browns hired as their first baseman a former Chicago sandlot star named Charles Comiskey. Comiskey, who was later to organize and own the Chicago White Sox, took over as Browns manager in 1885 and promptly led the team to four successive pennants, giving St. Louis a taste of the winning baseball the city would come to enjoy in the coming century.

In 1884 a third self-proclaimed major league

elbowed its way into the arena. This was the Union Association, destined for a one-year tenure before rounding third and disappearing from sight. It was a league of transient franchises, with teams dropping in and out all summer long, including among their number such urban centers as Wilmington, Delaware, and Altoona, Pennsylvania.

A member of the Union Association, and indeed its pennant winner, was the St. Louis Maroons, managed by Henry Lucas, nephew of John Lucas, who had owned the first St. Louis National League club. When the Union Association disintegrated, the National League voted a franchise to Henry Lucas and his Maroons.

St. Louis's second experience as a National League member lasted just two wretched and dismal seasons. In 1885 the Maroons finished at the bottom of the eight-team heap with a 36–72 record and in 1886 came in sixth with a 43–79 record. With Von Der Ahe's and Comiskey's Browns winning American Association pennants for St. Louis, the Maroons were unable to lay claim to enough fan allegiance to balance the books and, after the 1886 season, St. Louis dropped out of the National League for the second time.

In 1890, another major league was formed to compete with the National League and American Association. This was the ill-conceived Player's League, formed by players who had become disgruntled with the high-handed treatment accorded them by their employers, which included salary caps, arbitrary fines, and the detested reserve clause, that ball-and-chain clause in every contract that bound a player to the club for as long as the club determined. This assertion of independence lasted just a year, and when the year was over so was the Player's League.

Though it existed for only a single season, the Player's League was not without legacy. Forced to compete with two leagues—and with many of its star players having jumped to the new league—the already financially shaky American Association was weakened to the point of expiration and, after the 1891 season,

agreed to a merger with the stronger, more affluent National League. Four franchises from the disbanded circuit were absorbed by the National League, forming a single twelve-club structure. Included among the new members were Chris Von Der Ahe's St. Louis Browns. Thus, today's St. Louis Cardinals are lineal descendants of the old American Association team.

With Von Der Ahe himself managing in 1892, the Browns (as they were still known) finished eleventh. A year later, under new skipper Bill Watkins, the club raised itself to tenth place. In 1894, with yet another manager, George Miller, the club finished ninth. In 1895, this glacial upward progress was reversed by a 39–92 record and eleventh-place windup, a year in which Von Der Ahe astoundingly employed four managers, including himself for the final 14 games. The team included first baseman Roger Connor, who at the age of 38 was winding down a long career that was to see him hit 136 big-league home runs, which was the all-time record that Babe Ruth was to break in 1921. Connor (who was voted into the Hall of Fame in 1976) finished his 18-year career with St. Louis in 1897.

In 1896, Von Der Ahe, who seems to have anticipated George Steinbrenner's way with managers, employed Harry Diddlebock to manage; Harry lasted only 18 games and was replaced by Connor, who in turn was replaced by Tommy Dowd. The club finished eleventh. A year later the Browns hit rock bottom with a 29–102 record that was overseen by three more managers. In 1898 under Tim Hurst, later an umpire of some renown, the club was 39–111 and again finished dead last. This time the thud of another graveyard finish in St. Louis reverberated around the league. Tired of seeing a perpetually mismanaged, money-losing tail-ender in what should have been one of the league's strongest cities, the league, abetted by numerous creditors, forced Von Der Ahe to sell out.

After the 1898 season, the colorful and eccentric Von Der Ahe sold his team to one G.A. Gruner for $33,000. Gruner then sold it for ownership quickly became apparent. Dissatisfied with the attendance their solid and competitive team was drawing in Cleveland and feeling that St. Louis would be a more appreciative market, the Robisons switched most of their Cleveland stars to St. Louis.

This devious maneuver involved some of the game's reigning princes, among them right-hander Cy Young, then thirty-one years old and in the midst of building his legend; outfielder Jesse Burkett, twice a .400 hitter for Cleveland; and shortstop Bobby Wallace, good enough in his time to be known as "Mr. Shortstop." The team was managed by first baseman Patsy Tebeau. In return for these stars, the Cleveland team received some of the St. Louis culprits who, in addition to being short on talent, were so disgruntled by the move they

Roger Connor (1895–97), a big, hard-hitting first baseman who wound up his long career with St. Louis. His 233 triples are fifth most in baseball history.

$40,000 to the Robison brothers, Frank and Stanley, a couple of sharpies who personified the palmy, freewheeling ethics of 1890s baseball.

The Robison brothers, who had made their fortune operating streetcar companies in Fort Wayne, Indiana, and Cleveland, also owned Cleveland's entry in the league, then known as the Spiders. The dangers of such multiteam

Frank Robison, who, along with his brother Stanley, bought the St. Louis franchise for $40,000.

(26–15) and Burkett, who batted .402, second only to Philadelphia's Ed Delahanty, who led with a .408 average. It was Jesse's third .400 season in five years. Despite this high-altitude hitting, Burkett went around with a disposition sour enough to earn him the nickname "The Crab."

Hoping to erase all memories of Von Der Ahe's depressing Browns, the Robisons provided some bright new upholstery for their players. The new uniforms featured eye-pleasing red trim and red socks. According to legend, a female fan, upon seeing the new uniforms, exclaimed, "Oh, what a lovely shade of cardinal!" The remark was overheard by

Jesse ("The Crab") Burkett (1899–1901), who averaged .382 during his three years in St. Louis.

dragged the Spiders down to a never-matched level of ignominy. Cleveland finished the season with baseball's all-time worst record, 20–134—as close to embalming as any team has ever come.

While the fans in Cleveland were made miserable by the switch, in St. Louis they were delighted and proved it on opening day when some 18,000 of them—at the time the largest assemblage in St. Louis baseball history—filled the wooden stands of Sportsman's Park and stood behind ropes in the outfield.

In that year of rejuvenation, the club finished with a highly respectable 84–67 record, good enough for fifth place behind some exceptionally strong teams in Brooklyn, Boston, Philadelphia, and Baltimore. The St. Louis fans were able to enjoy and take pride in some stellar individual achievements, particularly from Young

Before the arrival of Honus Wagner, the Cardinals' Bobby Wallace (1899–1901, 1917–18) was baseball's "Mr. Shortstop."

The original Sportsman's Park.

sportswriter Willie McHale, who is generally credited with being the first to refer to the team in print as "the Cardinals." The nickname, which caught on quickly, was especially apt, since the crested, brightly colored bird is a familiar sight in the Midwest. The design of two cardinals perched on opposite ends of a recumbent baseball bat, one of the most familiar in the sports world, was added to the uniform several decades later.

In 1900, the National League trimmed its unwieldy twelve-team circuit to eight—Brooklyn, New York, Philadelphia, Boston, Chicago, Cincinnati, Pittsburgh, and St. Louis, an alignment that would remain intact until 1953. The Cardinals finished sixth that year, with Tebeau being replaced by Louie Heilbroner (the club's chief of concessions) toward the end of the season. The man Frank Robison wanted as manager was third baseman John McGraw, who had become available through the liquidation of the Baltimore club. McGraw, though he did play for the Cardinals in 1900 (in 99 games he batted .344), was not interested in managing in St. Louis.

The reason McGraw turned down the manager's job in St. Louis was because he was listening to the rumbles coming out of Ban Johnson's Western League, at the time baseball's top minor league. Johnson, the Western's president, had for years been planning to declare his circuit a major league and expand it across the country (and McGraw was hoping to secure for himself a managerial job in the East, which he eventually did, but it was in the National League, with the New York Giants). Having seen other fledgling leagues rise and fall, Ban had proceeded cautiously. He wanted franchises in the major cities—and if they were National League cities, so be it—and he wanted clubowners who were well-heeled and committed to baseball. When Johnson made his move in 1901, he changed the name of his circuit to the American League, anointed it a major league, and then, with his colleagues, went after the most essential element for success: players. And there was only one place to find them: the National League.

Thus began the most intense interleague war in baseball history, a comic opera of threats,

John McGraw (1900), who turned down the manager's job in St. Louis.

Cy Young (1899–1900). He found the St. Louis summer a bit too hot for his liking.

Lou Criger (1899–1900), who was Cy Young's favorite catcher. He caught the great man for 13 years, in Cleveland, St. Louis, and Boston.

insults, broken contracts, lawsuits, and players bouncing from one league to the other. The rivalry roared on for two years until the National League accepted the upstart league as a permanent fixture in baseball and agreed to a truce.

Of immeasurable help to the American League was its rival's arrogance as well as the older league's $2,400 salary limit. The newcomers began offering more sumptuous paydays and soon had some of the greatest players in the land knocking on the door and climbing through the window.

One of the first Cardinal players to switch leagues—and this was quite a coup for the Americans—was Cy Young, at the time the game's top pitcher. Cy, whose real name was Denton True Young (the Cy was short for "Cyclone," in honor of his fastball), had never been entirely happy pitching in the St. Louis summer heat and when the Boston American League club offered him more money and lower temperatures, the eminent pitcher went East, taking with him his favorite catcher, Lou Criger.

Under Patsy Donovan, who managed the club in 1901–03, the Cardinals finished fourth in 1901, leading the league with 39 home runs, the first of just five times a Cardinal team had ever led the league in this power category, the last time being 1940. In 1901, the year that baseball historians generally agree began the game's modern era, St. Louis's Jesse Burkett won the batting title with a .382 average, outfielder Emmet Heidrick batted .339, and Bobby Wallace .322. The team's big winners were right-handers Jack Harper (23–13), Jack Powell (19–19), and Willie Sudhoff (17–11). A year later, all six of these players were in the American League.

After the 1901 season, the American League folded its franchise in Milwaukee and moved it to St. Louis. The new team revived a familiar name by calling itself the Browns and took over Sportsman's Park as their home field. (The Cardinals were playing at what was now called Robison Field, the grounds at Vandeventer and Natural Bridge Avenues, where Henry Lucas's

Patsy Donovan (1900–03), Cardinal outfielder and manager.

National League club had begun playing in 1885.)

With Ban Johnson orchestrating the moves, the newly installed (and well-financed) Browns hit the Cardinal roster like a wave of locusts, stripping it bare of star players. Burkett, Wallace, Heidrick, Harper, Powell, and Sudhoff all jumped to the Browns, as did second baseman Dick Padden, while first baseman Dan McGann signed with Baltimore.

Patsy Donovan's rebuilt Cardinals struggled all summer in 1902, ending in sixth place, and, adding insult to injury, lost the attendance war

Jack Powell (1899–1901), the Cardinal ace who succumbed to American League money.

First baseman Dan McGann (1900–01), another jumper to the American League.

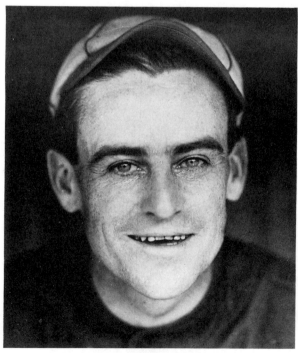

The gifted outfielder Mike Donlin (1899–1900), who made the switch to the new league.

Outfielder Homer Smoot (1902–06), who twice was a .300 hitter for the Cardinals.

Mordecai ("Three Finger") Brown (1903), the man that got away.
His lifetime ERA of 2.06 is the third lowest in baseball history.

with the crosstown Browns, 272,000 to 226,000. The only consolation for Cardinal fans that year was a .300-hitting outfield of skipper Donovan (.315) and rookies Homer Smoot (.311) and George Barclay (.300).

In 1903 a 43–94 record plunged the Cardinals into last place, costing Donovan his job (Patsy's .327 batting average was tops on the club, but the rest of the boys were unable to follow his good example).

The stability that came to baseball with the truce agreement between the two leagues came too late and brought too little to save the Cardinals season. One of the articles of agree-

ment stipulated that all of the league-jumping players would remain in place, which was a costly blow to the Cardinals and the rest of the National League clubs, who had lost the majority of players.

The Cardinals, however, had no one but themselves to blame for the loss of one of the premier pitching talents in baseball history. In 1903 the club had purchased from the minor leagues right-hander Mordecai Peter Centennial Brown (Centennial was for the year of his birth, 1876). Brown was better known as "Three Finger" because of the mangling his right hand had taken in a boyhood encounter with a threshing machine. The digital configurations left behind by the accident enabled Brown to put an unusual spin on his breaking pitches, and for years he was considered the league's only match for Christy Mathewson (Brown in fact bested Mathewson 14 of the 26 times they went to a decision). Combining his swooping curves with a live fastball, Brown was, for a half dozen years (1906–1911), nearly unbeatable.

The Cardinals, however, felt that the damaged hand would prevent Brown from becoming a winner (despite a 9–13 record and team-best 2.60 ERA) and on December 12, 1903, they made the colossal mistake of trading him to the Chicago Cubs, in return for right-hander Jack Taylor and young catcher Larry McLean. Taylor gave the Cardinals a couple of decent years and then was traded back to the Cubs. McLean played in just 27 games for St. Louis. Brown went on to first-magnitude stardom.

Infielder Dave Brain (1903–05). His 10 home runs for Boston in 1907 led the National League.

THE LEAN AND HUNGRY YEARS

THE FRACAS BETWEEN THE leagues had stripped the Cardinals of star players; the truce left them no better off, setting the tone for what were to be the dreariest ten years in the club's history. From 1904 through 1913, the team finished no better than fifth, doing that well only twice.

The manager in 1904, the year the National League went from a 140- to a 154-game schedule, was one of the 1890s' finest pitchers, Charles ("Kid") Nichols. Nichols had spent twelve years with the Boston club, winning 30 or more games for seven straight years. Now thirty-four years old, he still had enough left to post a 21–13 record. The following July, however, Nichols was canned as manager and waived to the Phillies. He was replaced by third baseman Jimmy Burke, who in turn was supplanted by co-owner Stanley Robison. The best that this concentration of brain power could produce was a sixth-place finish.

With Frank Robison taking less and less interest in the team—he had been bitterly disillusioned by the defection of his stars to the American League—his brother Stanley was assuming greater control. Stanley's managing the team for the last 57 games of the 1905 season was typical of his spirited approach. One old Stanley Robison chestnut that enlivened baseball gabfests around the turn of the century concerned the time he was walking through a hotel lobby when a woman stopped him and asked if he could tell her where the Browning Club met.

"I don't know, ma'am," Stanley told this devotee of the eminent English poet. "What league are they in?"

In 1906, 1907, and 1908 the Cardinals were managed by John McCloskey, known as "Honest John." Sterling character though he may have been, Honest John guided the team through the most wretched three consecutive years in their modern history, suffering through records of 52–98, 52–101, and 49–105, the

Longtime star first baseman Jake Beckley (1904–07), who ended his twenty-year big-league career with the Cardinals.

minors, pitched in one game, and then sent back to the minors, from where the Pittsburgh Pirates picked him up and for whom he went on to pitch until 1926, winning 194 games.

The 1907 club, finishing last, batted a feeble .232 and made life miserable for their pitchers by committing a whopping 349 errors, 87 more than their nearest rival in futility. Third baseman Bobby Byrne and shortstop Ed Holly combined for 111 errors, making the left side of the Cardinal infield a danger zone. Pitching doggedly all summer long for the team was a thirty-five-year-old right-hander with the resounding name of Ulysses Simpson Grant McGlynn, known as Stoney. In his only full big-league season, Stoney was 14–25, setting team records with his losses as well as with his 352 innings of work.

The 1908 club did the impossible—it made the previous year's edition look good. This was

George McBride (1905–06), who later had a long career playing shortstop for the Washington Senators.

latter two years representing the only 100-loss seasons the Cardinals have ever suffered. It was probably coincidence, but in September 1908, at the tail end of the team's 105-loss season, Frank Robison died of apoplexy.

The 1906 club batted .235 and totaled the lowest home run figure in Cardinal history—ten. Typifying the woes and missteps of the 1906 club, the Cardinals for the second time in three years let slip through the mesh a pitcher whose star would brighten another sky. This time it was Babe Adams, a twenty-four-year-old right-hander they had brought up from the

Bobby Byrne (1907–09), Cardinal third baseman. In 1907 Byrne teamed up with shortstop Ed Holly to commit 111 errors on the left side of the infield.

Bugs Raymond (1907–08), who was on the losing side of 11 shutouts in 1908. Bugs' taste for liquor got him traded to the New York Giants.

Tying Stoney McGlynn's club record for losses set the year before was right-hander Arthur ("Bugs") Raymond, a talented but wayward pitcher who was 15–25. Bugs was shut out 11 times during the season, which was enough to drive a man to drink, though according to legend Bugs didn't need much motivation for taking a nip. Tired of seeing their spitballing ace wobbling in on days when he was supposed to pitch, the Cardinals poured the problem East to the New York Giants in a postseason trade. John McGraw, who prided himself on handling difficult talent, got one decent year out of Bugs before giving up. Spending his last days in an alcoholic stupor, Raymond died in 1912 at the age of thirty.

In exchange for the unquenchable Raymond, the Cardinals received the man who would be their catcher and next manager, Roger Bresnahan. One of the great catchers of the era, indeed, a future Hall of Famer, the twenty-nine-year-old Bresnahan (who is credited with introducing shinguards for catchers) had managerial ambitions and McGraw decided to give him the opportunity with the Cardinals, who had dismissed McCloskey and were looking for a new skipper. (McGraw was willing to trade his number-one catcher because he had another one just as good coming along in Chief Meyers.)

In the four years he managed them, Bresnahan took the Cardinals from awfully bad to

the outfit that set team records for most losses (105), fewest runs (372), fewest hits (1,105), and lowest batting average (.223). In September the team virtually self-destructed, going only 7–27 for the month. Along with the Brooklyn club, which played to a 6–27 September, the team established the league record for losses in a single month.

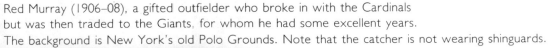

Red Murray (1906–08), a gifted outfielder who broke in with the Cardinals but was then traded to the Giants, for whom he had some excellent years. The background is New York's old Polo Grounds. Note that the catcher is not wearing shinguards.

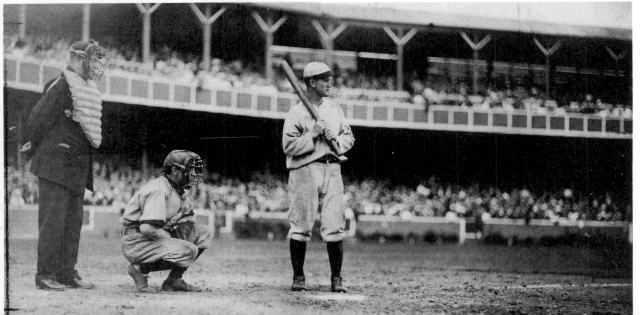

their fans to have become a vanished species—
the .300 hitter. The man who scaled that peak
was first baseman Ed Konetchy, whose .302
average made him the first Cardinal .300 hitter
since Homer Smoot in 1905.

In right-hander Bob Harmon and lefty Harry
("Slim") Sallee the club had a couple of pitchers
who were going to win consistently over the
next few years. Sallee was a blithe spirit who
demonstrated the quirkiness that seems to come
with being a big league southpaw. He was an
Ohio farmboy who was made nostalgic by the
sight of horsedrawn milk wagons, and frequently he was up at sunrise riding the wagons
and helping the drivers in their house deliver-
ies.

Another Cardinal who listened to special
voices was outfielder Steve Evans, who sounds
like he might have been a spiritual ancestor of
The Gashouse Gang. On one particularly blazing hot summer afternoon Steve sought the
only shade available, that which was cast by

Hall of Famer Roger Bresnahan (1909–12), who is
widely credited with inventing shinguards for catchers.

respectably bad, with a fifth-place finish in 1911
his best effort. The team's 75–74 record that
year was their first peep over .500 since 1901.

The team finished seventh in 1909 and
1910, with the sharp-tongued Bresnahan singe-
ing the umpires with sulphurous profanity,
provoking numerous suspensions from league
president John Heydler. The 1910 club returned to the Cardinals what had seemed to

Right-hander Fred Beebe (1906–09). He was 15–21
in the dreary 1909 season.

(ABOVE) Left-hander Johnny Lush (1907–10). His
best was 14–13 in 1910. (BELOW) Ed Konetchy
(1907–13), who gave the Cardinals some solid years
at first base.

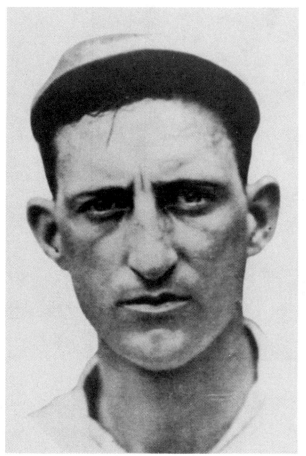

Southpaw Slim Sallee (1908–16), the country boy who liked to rise before dawn.

han's club was in the race until the beginning of August, and the St. Louis fans responded to this spirited play by coming out in record numbers—447,768, which remained the club mark until 1922. Harmon was the ace, going 23–16, while Sallee was 15–9. Konetchy's 38 doubles gave him the league lead, making him the first Cardinal to lead in an offensive department since Burkett's 1901 batting title.

With the death of Stanley Robison in 1911, ownership of the club passed to his niece, Mrs. Helen Britton, daughter of the late Frank Robison. An early advocate of women's rights, the attractive Mrs. Britton took active control of the club. To the discomfort of some of the

Bob Harmon (1909–13), who won 23 games for the Cardinals in 1911.

the edge of the right-field grandstand. In order to gain even this slight relief, however, he had to play inordinately deep, and several fly balls which ordinarily would have been caught fell in front of him for hits. After being chewed out between innings by Bresnahan, Evans somewhere found a Japanese paper parasol and, holding it over his head, trotted out to his position the next inning. When the umpire refused to allow the game to proceed with the right-fielder standing under an umbrella, Evans reluctantly folded it up and threw it away, yelling at the umpire, "How would you like to stand out in this sun without an umbrella?" To which the perspiring ump yelled back, "Dammit, I *am* standing out in this sun without an umbrella."

The 1911 club came in fifth, 22 games back, but that didn't tell the whole story. Bresna-

Mike Mowrey played third base for the Cardinals from 1909 to 1913.
Like Evans, Mowrey jumped to the Federal League in 1914.

hard-nosed National League owners, the strong-minded Mrs. Britton insisted on attending league councils, where her presence caused a cutback in profanity and a reduction of cigar smoke.

The team's 1911 showing had raised hopes for the 1912 season, but when the Cardinals broke an axle with a 7–20 June and creaked into sixth place, there was keen disappointment in the executive suite. Bresnahan was summoned to Mrs. Britton's home for a post-season post-mortem. When the owner began voicing some criticisms of the team's perfor-

(TOP LEFT) Shortstop Arnold Hauser (1910–13).
(BOTTOM LEFT) Steve Evans (1909–13), the man who took an umbrella out to right field. Evans joined the Federal League in 1914.
(BELOW) Right-hander Bill Steele (1910–14). He was 16–19 in 1911.

mance, an angry Bresnahan responded loudly, wanting to know "what the hell any god-damned woman can tell me about baseball." The lady was incensed. When Bresnahan walked out of the house, he might as well have kept on going—he was on his way out of St. Louis.

Because Bresnahan was in the midst of a five-year contract (at the rate of $10,000 per year, generous for the time) there was some squabbling over money, which wasn't settled until the following June, when Roger, who had been sitting it out, was sold to the Cubs.

The man Mrs. Britton selected to succeed Bresnahan was the club's thirty-four-year-old second baseman, Miller Huggins. After earning a law degree, the five-feet-six-inch Huggins decided to give professional baseball a shot. Cincinnati-born, he broke into the majors with his hometown team in 1904. After six years with the Reds, he was traded to the Cardinals in 1910. The little second baseman's best year with the Cardinals was .304 in 1912.

Huggins' first year as Cardinal manager ended in the dustbin of last place, with attendance slipping to 203,000. (For what consolation it afforded, the crosstown Browns also bottomed-out that year, the only time that both St. Louis teams had the basement view in the same season.) The skipper tried to set a good example with a .286 batting average, while the team's leading batter was outfielder Rebel Oakes at .291. (Oakes was a Louisiana native and in those years there were still enough live memories for a Southern-born player to be called "Rebel.") Sallee managed an 18–15 record for a club that was 51–99, and the Cardinals brought up twenty-one-year-old right-hander Bill Doak, who broke in with a 2–8 record but who was soon to become one of the team's fine pitchers.

Some old memories were stirred in 1914; not only was war breaking out in Europe, but there was another one erupting in major league baseball. Reminiscent of the advent of the American League and players being seduced by larger contracts, a new, self-proclaimed major league calling itself the Federal League shouldered its

Mrs. Helene Britton assumed ownership of the Cardinals with the death of her uncle in 1911.

way onto the landscape. This jerry-built concoction was destined to last only two years, but its shrapnel punctured a lot of hides.

The new, eight-team league planted one of its clubs in St. Louis; so, in 1914, the city found itself being entertained by three major league teams. While the rosters of some teams were hit hard by the Federal League predators, the Cardinals weren't one of them, their principal defectors being outfielders Steve Evans and Rebel Oakes. The incursion of the Feds hurt somewhat at the gate, but the 1914 Cardinals had their most artistically successful season of the new century, driving to a third-place finish.

Huggins' team was in the race until late August, but then a fast finish by baseball's first "Miracle" team—the Boston Braves, who had

Miller Huggins, who played second base for the Cardinals from 1910 to 1916 and managed the club from 1913 through 1917. He later managed the New York Yankees, winning six pennants in the 1920s.

Outfielder Ennis Talmadge Oakes (1910–13) of Homer, Louisiana. They called him "Rebel."

22

Bill Doak (1913–24, 1929), one of the top Cardinal pitchers of the World War I era. He was a 20-game winner in 1914 and again in 1920. His 32 shutouts rank second in club history to Bob Gibson's 56.

Dan Griner (1912–16). The right-hander suffered through 22 losses in 1913.

Ivy Wingo (1911–14). The catcher batted .300 in 1914.

Dots Miller, who played around the infield for the Cardinals from 1914 through 1919.

Outfielder Owen Wilson (1914–16). His 36 triples for the Pirates in 1912 remains the major league record.

been in last place on July 4—threw up a cloud of dust and when it settled the Cardinals were third, 13 games out. With the team in the race for much of the summer, the year's attendance of 256,099 was disappointing and indicated the inroads made by the Federal League club, the St. Louis Sloufeds.

Huggins ran three solid starters through the league in his pursuit of the pennant—young Doak spitballed his way to a 20–6 record and league-leading 1.72 earned run average (he was the first Cardinal pitcher to lead in this cate-gory), Sallee was 18–17, and young right-hander Pol Perritt 16–13 (Perritt was sold to the Giants after the season for some needed cash). The staff ERA of 2.38 was the best in the league, but could not offset a team batting average of .248, which was fifth best. Two players obtained in a trade with the Pirates led the team offense—first baseman Dots Miller at .290 and 88 RBIs, and outfielder Owen Wilson with 73 RBIs. Wilson was the man who in 1912 set one of baseball's untouchable records when he hit 36 triples for Pittsburgh.

Catcher Frank Snyder (1912–19, 1927), known as ''Pancho.''

In 1915 the Cardinals had a curious year—they led the league with 590 runs and a .254 batting average but finished sixth, keenly disappointing those whose expectations had been piqued by the strong showing in 1914. Adding to the club's woes this year was a sizzling three-way pennant race in the Federal League, in which the St. Louis entry was involved (they finished second by percentage points), and this helped siphon off some more Cardinal attendance.

Huggins got some solid hitting from young catcher Frank Snyder (.298) and outfielder Tommy Long, who led the league—and set an all-time club record—with 25 triples, batting .294.

Altogether, 1915 would have been a forgettable year for the Cardinals if not for what took place on September 10. Finishing the game at shortstop for the team was nineteen-year-old Rogers Hornsby, brought up from Denison, Texas, in the Western Association, where he had batted .277.

The man who was going to become the first St. Louis Cardinal superstar, as well as the greatest of all right-handed hitters, was born in Winters, Texas, on April 27, 1896. The name of his birthplace was ironically apt, for Hornsby was by all accounts a cold man, dispassionate and without sentiment. Teammates described his gray eyes as "the coldest" they had ever seen. One newspaperman described Hornsby at the plate staring out at the pitcher "with a gunfighter's calculating eyes." It all seemed appropriate—the product of the waning Texas frontier, who would do his unprecedented and unequaled hitting in what was then big league baseball's frontier outpost, evoked comparisons with a gunfighter. Hornsby's bat was capable of the most flawless sharpshooting in history. He would bat .424 in 1924, which remains the twentieth century's landmark achievement of man against pitched ball.

Oddly enough, it wasn't Hornsby's hitting that attracted Cardinal scout Bob Connery in 1915. Because they were unable to compete with the wealthier teams for minor league talent (most minor league teams were independently owned in those years and subsisted primarily on developing talent and selling it to the majors), the Cardinal talent hunters patrolled the less traveled byways. In the spring of 1915, Connery arrived in Denison, Texas. There he was taken with the club's shortstop (Hornsby didn't become a full-time second baseman until 1920).

Rogers Hornsby in 1918. A star on the rise.

"Contrary to reports," Connery said later, "I wasn't so much impressed with his hitting. What I saw was a loose gangling kid, with a good pair of hands, a strong arm, and a world of pep and life on the field. I think I noted then that he was a personality, and I found myself unconsciously attracted to him."

Hornsby was indeed a sharply defined personality. Along with his handsome good looks and dimpled smile, he was also, as became more and more evident with stardom, a brutally frank and outspoken man, at times contemptuously so. Where Ty Cobb, the only man in history to outhit him (.367 lifetime to .358), snarled and sneered, Hornsby was blunt and sarcastic and tactless. Some players disliked "The Rajah," others worshiped him, but no one ignored him. "When Rogers stepped into the cage during batting practice," one player recalled, "it was like when Ruth stepped in—

everybody stopped what they were doing to watch him."

Connery followed the Denison club for about a week after the season opened, and then deciding that Hornsby was "a good prospect, a lad who had a chance," bought him for the Cardinals for $500. Breaking into 18 games with St. Louis that September, the boy batted .246.

In the spring of 1916, Connery took Hornsby aside and changed the youngster's batting stance. Rogers had been batting from a crouch, choking up on the bat. Connery moved him as far back in the box as legally possible and had him grip the bat closer to the knob. It became one of the most distinctive stances in baseball. No other top star ever stood so far away from the plate, and with his flawless power swing Hornsby was able to sweep the entire strike zone, sending blistering line drives in all directions.

Despite a .313 batting average from Hornsby in his first full season (the rookie split his time between third base and shortstop), the Cardinals tied for last place in 1916.

Toward the end of the 1916 season, Mrs. Britton decided she had had enough baseball and put the team up for sale. Huggins was an interested buyer and set out to obtain the necessary backing—the asking price was $375,000. But before the skipper could present his proposition, Mrs. Britton sold the team to a syndicate of wealthy St. Louis baseball fans that had been organized by her legal adviser, James C. Jones.

Soon after the completion of the purchase, Jones convened a meeting of seven of the city's top sports editors and baseball writers. He was interested in hiring someone to run the team and wanted the advice of experts on whom to select. He supplied each of the seven men with a slip of paper, asked them to write a name on it and drop it into the hat he would pass around the room. The results of this informal nominating process were unanimous, the same name being written on every slip: Branch Rickey. With so total an endorsement in his hands,

Jones immediately went out and offered Rickey the presidency of the St. Louis Cardinals.

The man who was going to have more impact on the game of baseball than any non-player was at the moment the business manager of the St. Louis Browns. Phil Ball, the owner of the Browns, was reluctant to let Rickey go and after the parties took the dispute to court it was settled in Rickey's favor. So in 1917 the thirty-six-year-old Wesley Branch Rickey took over as president of the Cardinals.

Rickey was born on a farm near Lucasville, Ohio, on December 20, 1881. Always a bright kid—he was studying math and Latin and rhetoric on his own before going off to college—he graduated with honors from Ohio Wesleyan and went into teaching, first at Allegheny College in western Pennsylvania, then at Delaware College in Ohio. A scholar-athlete, Rickey played semipro baseball in the summer and a brand of professional football in the fall (a broken leg put an end to his football-playing in 1902).

A catcher, the tough, broad-shouldered Rickey entered pro ball in 1903. In 1906 he reached the big leagues with the Browns, batting .284 in 64 games, the busiest year of his brief playing career. He was then traded to the Yankees, for whom he got into 57 games in 1907, batting .182. That was about the extent of his playing, though he did earn a dubious line in the record books on June 28, 1907, when 13 Washington Senators stole successfully while he was catching.

Rickey managed the Browns from September 6, 1913, through the 1915 season, then served as the club's vice-president and business manager in 1916 before moving into the Cardinal job.

Rickey remains one of baseball's truly impressive characters: athlete, intellectual, innovator, visionary. He could be an oratorical spellbinder, peppering his rhetoric with Biblical quotations and citations from the classics. He was eloquent and bombastic, a windbag to some, to others a prophet. He was as shrewd an evaluator of talent as there has ever been in the game. To some he was excruciatingly parsimonious and a hypocrite, to others virtually a surrogate father. He accepted baseball for what it was—a business, which offended some romantics. It was Rickey who was to lead a reluctant baseball establishment to its noblest moment, the breaking of the game's noxious color barrier, when he signed Jackie Robinson to a professional contract in 1945. That was to be the culminating achievement of Rickey's career, a career that didn't start occupying high ground until 1917, when he took over the St. Louis Cardinals front office.

The Cardinals made it to third place in 1917, only the second time they had finished as high since 1901. The most notable Cardinal by far was young Hornsby, who batted .327 (second in the league to Edd Roush's .341) and led with 17 triples and a .484 slugging average, the first of nine slugging titles he would take.

Despite a relatively successful season in 1917, Miller Huggins had done a lot of sulking. The little manager had never gotten over the disappointment of not being given a chance to bid for ownership of the team. So, when an offer came from New York Yankee owner Ja-

Former New York Giant ace Red Ames, who pitched for the Cardinals from 1915 to 1919. He won 15 games in 1917.

Pitcher Lee Meadows (1915–19). He had his best years later with the Pirates.

cob Ruppert to manage in New York, Huggins accepted and went to the big city, where he managed for 11 years, winning six pennants, before his untimely death in September 1929 at the age of fifty.

Huggins' successor was Jack Hendricks, who had had a brief career as an outfielder with the Giants, Cubs, and Senators at the turn of the century. Jack, who later managed the Cincinnati Reds for six years, lasted just the 1918 season in St. Louis, and it was not a memorable one—for the fifth time since 1901, the club finished in last place (which they have not done since). Mercifully for Jack and his beleaguered men, the Cardinals suffered through only 129 games that year when, because of the World

Outfielder Burt Shotton (1919–23) takes a cut in batting practice.

War, the baseball schedule terminated on Labor Day.

In 1919 the Cardinals' new manager was Rickey himself, taking over the dugout while at the same time holding onto the club presidency. Though the club finished seventh, obviously Rickey the president forgave Rickey the manager, for Branch was to manage the team into the 1925 season.

Still dividing his time between second, short, and third, Hornsby's .318 average fell three points short of earning him his first batting title. Rogers, like everyone else, was still punching away at a ball that had all the resiliency of a pumpkin. That was about to change. The lively ball was on the way, and it would give baseball a permanent face lift.

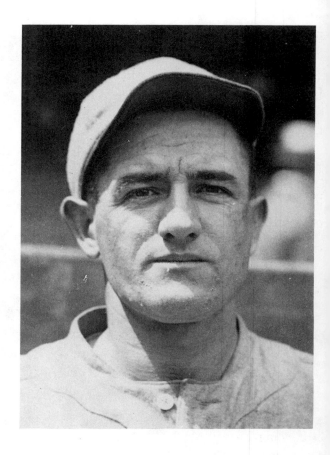

Milt Stock, who played second and third for the Cardinals from 1919 through 1923. He had 204 hits in 1920, batting .319.

26 St – NY

28 NY – St

30 PHIL – St

31 STL – Ph

34 St – DET

42 St   NY

43 NY   St

44 STLC – STB

46 St   BOS

49 St   NY

64 St   NY

67 St   BOST

68 St   DET

82   ST   MIL
85   St   KC
87   MIN - ST
04   Bost - ST
06   ST - DET

18 - Pennt

13 - 5   world Seri

T·H·R·E·E

A NEW ERA

WITH THE INTRODUCTION of the lively ball in 1920, baseball was launched into the most hit-happy decade in its history. Line drives crackled like lightning bolts and offensive records were broken year after year. For the Cardinals, who went into it as the only National League team not to have won a pennant since the formation of the two-league structure in 1901, the decade would see them building toward a point where they were to become the most successful team in the league for the better part of twenty years.

In the American League, the man was Babe Ruth, whose breathtaking power hitting made him seem like a new species on earth. In the National League, it was Rogers Hornsby, who put on a sustained machine-gun attack that set record after record, some of them seemingly destined to remain in place for the rest of the century. Beginning in 1920, Hornsby ran off six consecutive batting titles and six consecutive slugging titles, a dominance not seen in the league before or since. It was a hitter's decade and the cold and humorless "Rajah" was the best of the best.

In 1920, Sam Breadon bought a majority interest in the Cardinals. He demoted Rickey to vice-president but retained him as manager. Born in New York's Greenwich Village in 1879, Breadon came to be known as "Lucky Sam," but in his case it was "luck" flowing in the wake of hard work, initiative, imagination, and shrewd judgment when it came to taking chances.

Sam Breadon.

The twenty-four-year-old Breadon had been earning $125 per month as a bank teller in New York when he heeded a familiar siren call and headed out West (to St. Louis) in 1903. The trip was spurred by a friend who was starting a garage and automobile agency. The automobile industry barely had all four wheels touching the ground at this time, but the canny Breadon, with a perceptive look into the future, soon had a partnership in his own agency, "The Western Automobile Co."

Coaxed by a friend, Breadon, who was not really a baseball man, became a small part of the syndicate that bought the Cardinals from Mrs. Britton. When the syndicate began hurting for money, Sam advanced a loan, and from there on was gradually drawn in deeper and deeper until he became majority owner.

"Once I was elected president," he said, "I really became vitally interested in the club, and baseball in general." He was determined to employ his "good business sense" to making the Cardinals "a winner, not only on the field, but in the box office."

The first thing Sam did was persuade a reluctant Phil Ball to allow the Cardinals to share Sportsman's Park with his Browns on a tenant basis. The two hard-nosed owners agreed on a rent of $35,000. On June 6, 1920, the Cardinals played their last game in ramshackle Robison Field and moved into the park that was to become as indelibly a part of their history as the famous Redbird logo.

Breadon then turned around and sold the Robison Field real estate for $275,000, using part of this money to launch one of baseball's most significant innovations—the farm system.

The concept of a farm system began forming in Branch Rickey's mind in 1919. To some people it was an inspired idea, but to Rickey it was a case of developing desperately needed resources. The wealthiest teams (in the National League this meant the New York Giants) were always able to outbid everyone else for the choice minor league players. Success, of course, begat success. The best players enabled a team to make the most money; money allowed them to hire the most scouts to scour the country and discover top young talent. The Cardinals' scouting department was essentially a sharp-eyed ivory hunter named Charley Barrett, one of the best, but the tireless Charley could cover only so much ground.

(LEFT) Rogers Hornsby. Between 1921 and 1925, "Rajah" hit for an average of .402. (OPPOSITE RIGHT) Hornsby obliging a photographer before a game.

"Starting the Cardinal farm system was no sudden stroke of genius," Rickey said. "It was a case of necessity being the mother of invention. We lived a precarious existence. We would trade one player for four, and then maybe sell one who developed for a little extra cash with which to buy a few minor leaguers others passed up."

In addition, Rickey's own reputation as a judge of talent sometimes became a handicap. If the Cardinal sharpshooter expressed interest in a minor league player, the minor league clubowner might notify one of the wealthier teams, knowing that Rickey's interest in the player would pique theirs. Some clubs were known to quickly outbid Rickey for the player sight unseen, satisfied that Branch's interest was a sufficient scouting report.

"That kind of thing drove me mad," Rickey said. "We were scouting players for other clubs to pick up. I pondered long on it, and finally concluded that if we were too poor to buy, we would have to raise our own."

The wholesale development of baseball talent began in 1919 when the Cardinals bought a share of the Houston club of the Texas League. Soon after that, they acquired the Fort Smith, Arkansas, team of the Western Association, and following that came a half-interest in the Syracuse franchise of the International League (two years later the Cardinals bought out the other half and in 1927 transferred their interest to Rochester, which became their number-one farm club).

As the success of their minor league ventures increased, Rickey began expanding until the Cardinals controlled what amounted to a baseball empire. During World War II, when he was running the Brooklyn Dodgers, Rickey sent his scouts all over the country with orders to sign any youngster who showed the merest glint of talent, and thus when the war was over the other National League clubs found themselves faced with an abundantly stocked Brooklyn farm system that began producing players for six pennant-winning teams in ten years. Similarly, Rickey was able to exploit the conditions of an economically depressed country

in the 1930s by signing young, baseball-hungry players for salaries as little as $60 per month. At this subsistence level, the Cardinals could afford to sign any youngster who possessed what Rickey called "the God-given talents"—running speed and a strong arm.

Once the farm system began producing talented players in the mid-1920s, virtually every Cardinal star for thirty years was to rise from it, with other big-league teams featuring players from the overflow (Rickey reportedly received 25 percent of the selling price for every player sold out of the organization, an arrangement that made him a wealthy man). Because of the abundance of talent in the system, it often took five or six years for a player to make his way up through it, but when he had finally survived the Darwinian selection process, he was a fully trained, fully prepared big leaguer, imbued with the fundamental strengths that Rickey insisted be taught every player. Consequently, those champion Cardinal teams, particularly the pennant winners of the 1940s, played with the unity of a single instinct, with an élan, an intensity, and a craving (another Rickey policy was to keep them underpaid and hungry) that has seldom been seen on a baseball diamond.

They graduated to the Cardinals from the top farm clubs at Rochester, Sacramento, Houston, Columbus (Ohio), having played their way up from such way stations as Union Springs, Alabama; Paducah, Kentucky; Grand Island, Nebraska; New Iberia, Louisiana; Greensburg, Pennsylvania; Caruthersville, Missouri; Pine Bluff, Arkansas, and many others scattered across the country like colonial outposts, whose rough-surfaced ball parks are long since gone, paved over for highways, shopping malls, subdivisions. They were the rich and fertile soil from which rose the sprouts that flourished as the Cardinal empire.

While the Cardinals were now in the business of raising their own players, they had the National League's best playing second base for them. Rogers Hornsby began in 1920 six consecutive years of the most torrid hitting in baseball history. He took the first of his six straight batting titles with a .370 average (the lowest of the six), becoming the first St. Louis National League player since Jesse Burkett in 1901 to lead in batting. He also led in slugging (.559), hits (218), runs batted in (94), doubles (44), and total bases (329). He was twenty-four years old and just getting warmed up.

Bill Doak was a 20-game winner for the second time (20–12) and the club broke in a newcomer in right-hander Jesse Haines, who was 13–20. Haines, who featured a knuckleball, was a twenty-six-year-old rookie who was beginning what was going to be an 18-year career in a Cardinal uniform, longer than any other Redbird pitcher. By the time he retired in 1937 he would have won 210 games and become known as "Pop."

Also playing well for the 1920 Cardinals was twenty-four-year-old outfielder Austin McHenry, who batted .282, fielded superbly, and was looked upon by Rickey as a coming star.

The premature death of outfielder Austin McHenry (1918–22) at the age of twenty-seven aborted what Branch Rickey said would have been a "brilliant career."

Though the team led the league with a .289 batting average and set an all-time club record with 96 triples, it finished in a disappointing fifth-place tie with the Chicago Cubs. A year later, however, Rickey led them to a 28–6 mid-August to mid-September drive that landed the team in third place with an 87-66 record, their best showing of the modern era, finishing seven games out of first place.

Hornsby climbed to .397 for his second straight batting crown, also leading in slugging (.639), hits (235), doubles (44), triples (18), RBIs (126), runs (131), and total bases (378). The Hornsby aura was by now so mesmerizing that Giants owner Charles Stoneham offered the Cardinals $300,000 for him. Wisely, Breadon turned it down.

"Sure it was tempting," Sam said. "But we wanted a winner in St. Louis and we knew that Hornsby was the guy who could bring it to us."

The National League batted .289 in 1921, with the Cardinals on top with a .308 team mark. Rickey had McHenry at .350 (third best in the league), first baseman Jack Fournier .343, outfielders Jack Smith and Les Mann at .328 each, catcher Vern Clemons .320, and third baseman Milt Stock .307. These averages were typical of the rousing hitting that went on in both leagues throughout the decade.

Haines topped the staff in 1921 with an 18–12 record, followed by Doak at 15–6 and a league-leading 2.58 earned run average.

The 1922 Cardinals finished third again, tied with Pittsburgh, and set a new club attendance record with 536,988 paid customers. Most of those fans came out to see Hornsby, and the league's most potent batsman seldom disappointed. Rogers put together one of his mightiest seasons ever. In 1922 the outspoken, frosty-eyed Texan, on his way to a Triple Crown year, set some bruising, man-size league records. With these figures Hornsby set modern National League standards: .401 batting average, .722 slugging average, 141 runs scored, 250 hits, 42 home runs, 152 runs batted in, and 450 total bases. While the total base record still stands, all of the other marks were broken be-

38

(BELOW) Jesse Haines (1920–37), who pitched longer for the Cardinals than any hurler in club history. His 210 Redbird victories are second only to Bob Gibson's 251.

(ABOVE) Jack Fournier (1920–22). A good-hitting first baseman, Jack rapped out a .343 average in 1921, but the Cardinals had to trade him to make way for Sunny Jim Bottomley.

(OPPOSITE RIGHT) Rogers Hornsby, tool in hand.

fore the decade was out—some by Hornsby himself—which is further indication of the monumental hitting propensities unleashed by the lively ball. (With George Sisler batting .420 for the Browns that year, St. Louis was the hitting capital of baseball.) Hornsby also established an all-time Cardinal record with a 33-game hitting streak.

The team batted .301, which was only good enough for third best in the league that year. A late-season addition was a twenty-two-year-old first baseman named Jim Bottomley, soon to become second to Hornsby as the team's chief knocker. In 37 games, Bottomley, whose genial disposition got him the nickname "Sunny Jim," batted .325. He was the first of the major stars to rise from the young farm system.

The Cardinals were struck by a pair of tragedies in 1922. At about the time the club was preparing for spring training in February, backup catcher Bill ("Pickles") Dillhoefer succumbed to pneumonia. He was twenty-seven years old. In June, Rickey noticed that McHenry, one of his personal favorites, was not getting to fly balls that normally he would have. The young outfielder had been complaining of headaches, so Rickey took him to a doctor. McHenry was diagnosed as having a brain tumor (the gritty youngster was batting .303, despite his suffering). On November 27, McHenry, for whom Rickey had forecast stardom, died, two months after his twenty-seventh birthday.

After a pair of strong third-place showings, the Cardinals disappointed their fans with a dip to fifth place in 1923. The club's sluggish performance cost a 200,000 drop in attendance, despite the heavy hitting of Hornsby and rookie Bottomley. Rogers led the league with a .384 average, playing in just 106 games because of illness and a September suspension by Rickey. The suspension was imposed after Hornsby left the club pleading illness, despite a doctor's report suggesting he was fit for duty. As one who lived closer to his maker than most men, Rickey, who at one point exchanged punches with his star in the clubhouse, declared he "would overlook unprintable names which Hornsby" had called him.

Sunny Jim Bottomley, with a personality that was the antithesis of the prickly Hornsby's, battered National League pitching for a .371 average in his first full go-around, finishing second in the batting race to his illustrious teammate.

A rarity occurred on July 23 in a double-header at Braves Field, Boston. Rickey gave rookie right-hander Johnny Stuart his first start of the year and Johnny came through. Following a smooth, three-hit, 11–1 victory in the first game, he promptly received his second start of the year, in the second game of the double-

Sunny Jim Bottomley (1922–32).

ing of opposing pitchers helped the club to a .290 team average, second best in the league. Nevertheless, they finished in sixth place.

For Bottomley, it was a satisfying season, with a .316 average, 111 RBIs, and one afternoon of delectable mayhem at Brooklyn's Ebbets Field that is still in the record books. The date was September 16 and the final score was St. Louis 17 and Brooklyn 3, with 12 of the Cardinal runs being driven in by Sunny Jim (still the single greatest one-game RBI performance in major league history). Bottomley did it this way: two-run single in the first inning; one-run double in the second inning; grand slam home run in the fourth; two-run homer in the sixth; two-run single in the seventh; one-run single in the ninth. Adding an extra dollop of interest to the display was that the old record of 11 RBIs in one game had been held by the man then managing the Dodgers, Wilbert Robinson, who had set it when he was playing with Baltimore in the 1890s.

William ("Pickles") Dillhoefer (1919–21), who died at the age of twenty-seven.

header. Stuart, who volunteered for the iron-man stunt, won this one as well, 6–3. He finished the season with a 9–5 record, was 9–11 the following year, then faded from the big leagues.

Haines was 20–13 in 1923 and a slim left-hander named Bill Sherdel was 15–13, after which the pitching flattened out.

Despite some scintillating personal achievements, the 1924 season was an even more dismal disappointment for Cardinal fans than 1923 had been. But this was the year, under those hot Missouri skies of long ago, that Rogers Hornsby scaled the Mount Everest of twentieth-century batting averages with a mark of .424, a figure of such regal superiority that no one has since come close to approaching it. He achieved it by coming to the plate 536 times and collecting 227 hits. This prodigious bash-

Outfielder Max Flack (1922–25), who was obtained from the Cubs between games of a doubleheader in a trade for Cliff Heathcote. Both men played for each team that day.

"I could've walked him when he started getting close," Robinson said later.

"But you figured you'd give him a sporting shot at it, eh?" a writer asked.

"No," Robinson said. "I lost track of how many he had."

For Jesse Haines it was a wretched season—8-19—but at Sportsman's Park on July 17 he made a bit of history of his own. On that summer afternoon in St. Louis, Haines became the first Cardinal pitcher in the twentieth century to toss a no-hitter, putting the kibosh on the Braves, 5–0.

Two days later, rookie right-hander Herman ("Hi") Bell became the last National League pitcher to pitch two complete game victories in one day, winning by scores of 6–1 and 2–1. The victims were the Boston Braves, who managed just six hits in the doubleheader. Underlining Bell's effort was the fact that he was 3–8 for the season, pitching primarily in relief.

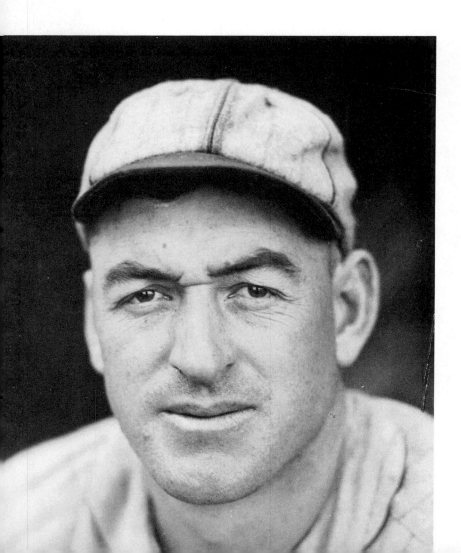

Tempering the disappointing season for the Cardinals was the increasing production of their farm system. Breaking into the lineup in 1924 were outfielders Chick Hafey and Taylor Douthit and infielder Les Bell, part of the team that in two years was going to rock the city.

The winds of change were spinning the vanes of Cardinal baseball in 1925, pointing them off to new, promising directions. Bell was the regular at third base, Hafey in right field. Hafey was a player who had the highest admiration from teammates and opponents alike. One of the first players to wear glasses on the field (teammate George Toporcer was the first bespectacled infielder), the right-handed-batting Hafey was said to hit the hardest line drives in the league; he was also said to possess the strongest throwing arm in baseball.

On May 23, Rickey engineered a good swap when he obtained catcher Bob O'Farrell from the Cubs for catcher Mike Gonzales and infielder Howard Freigau.

Thirty-eight games into the 1925 schedule the Cardinals were 13–25 and obviously going nowhere. When Breadon heard that ticket sales for the club's Sunday May 31 game were practically nil, the owner took the night train for Pittsburgh, where the Cardinals were playing. An owner can tolerate many slumps, but not one at the box office. Sam arrived in Pittsburgh and told Rickey a dugout change was being made: Rickey was out and Hornsby was in, with Rickey staying on as general manager, if Branch wanted to. Rickey wanted to continue as manager, a job he enjoyed, but which many of his players suggested he wasn't very good at, bringing too much "theory" to his tactical decisions. So Rickey handed in his lineup card and moved full-time into the front office. In a somewhat hasty move, he sold his stock in the club to Breadon, who transferred it to Hornsby, endorsing the new manager's $50,000 note for it.

Right-hander Herman ("Hi") Bell (1924, 1926–27, 1929–30). In 1924 he pitched and won both ends of a doubleheader, the last National Leaguer to do so. He was, however, primarily a relief pitcher.

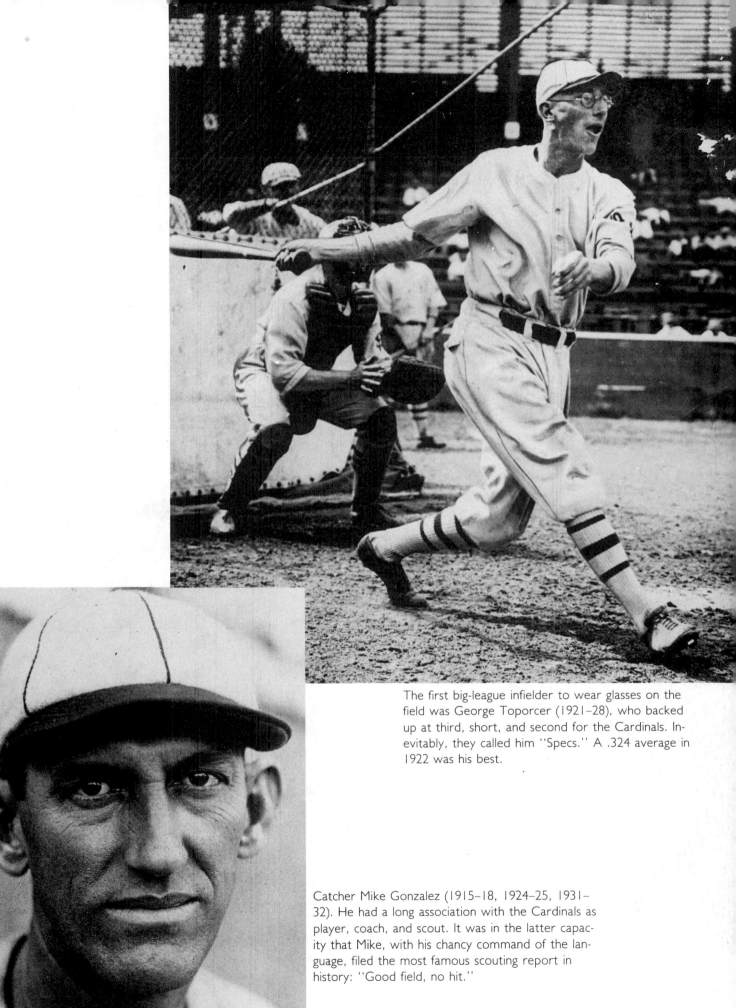

The first big-league infielder to wear glasses on the field was George Toporcer (1921–28), who backed up at third, short, and second for the Cardinals. Inevitably, they called him "Specs." A .324 average in 1922 was his best.

Catcher Mike Gonzalez (1915–18, 1924–25, 1931–32). He had a long association with the Cardinals as player, coach, and scout. It was in the latter capacity that Mike, with his chancy command of the language, filed the most famous scouting report in history: "Good field, no hit."

Skipper Hornsby manning the dugout in 1926.

In 1926 the Cardinals went to spring training in San Antonio. On the first day Hornsby called a meeting.

"I'll never forget it," Les Bell said. "He got us all together and in that blunt way of his said, 'If there's anybody in this room who doesn't think we're going to win the pennant, go upstairs and get your money and go home, because we don't want you around here.' "

Despite Hornsby's confidence and resolve, the Cardinals started slowly. In the middle of May they were seventh, in early June they had struggled into fifth place. Then the club engineered a couple of deals that were going to make a difference. On June 14, the eve of the trading deadline, St. Louis obtained outfielder Billy Southworth from the Giants in exchange for outfielder Heinie Mueller. The thirty-three-

Billy Southworth, who played in the Cardinal outfield in 1926 and 1927, then managed the team in 1929 and again from 1940 through 1945.

Under Hornsby, the team played better ball, posting a 64–51 record and ending up in fourth place. The skipper batted .403, hit 39 home runs, and drove in 143 runs to take his second Triple Crown. His .756 slugging average set a league standard that remains to this day. For Rogers it was now six batting and six slugging titles in a row, a dominance unprecedented and unequaled in league annals. Over the last five years (1921–25) the Cardinals' clockwork hitter had averaged .402. Bottomley was runner-up to Hornsby in 1925 with a .367 average and set a team record with three grand slams (tied by Keith Hernandez in 1977).

year-old Southworth, a good journeyman player, coughed up a .320 batting average as he took over right field, giving the club, along with Hafey in left and Douthit in center, an excellent outfield.

Eight days later, the club made another transaction, one that would lead to one of baseball's pinnacle moments that October. For the waiver price, the Cardinals acquired Grover Cleveland Alexander from the Cubs. Successor to Christy Mathewson as the league's premier pitcher, the now thirty-nine-year-old Alex had been fighting a sad and losing battle with epilepsy and alcoholism. When the no-nonsense

Les Bell (1923–27). The Cardinal third baseman had his best season in the 1926 pennant year, hitting .325.

Grover Cleveland Alexander (1926–29). He recorded one of baseball's most famous strikeouts in the 1926 World Series.

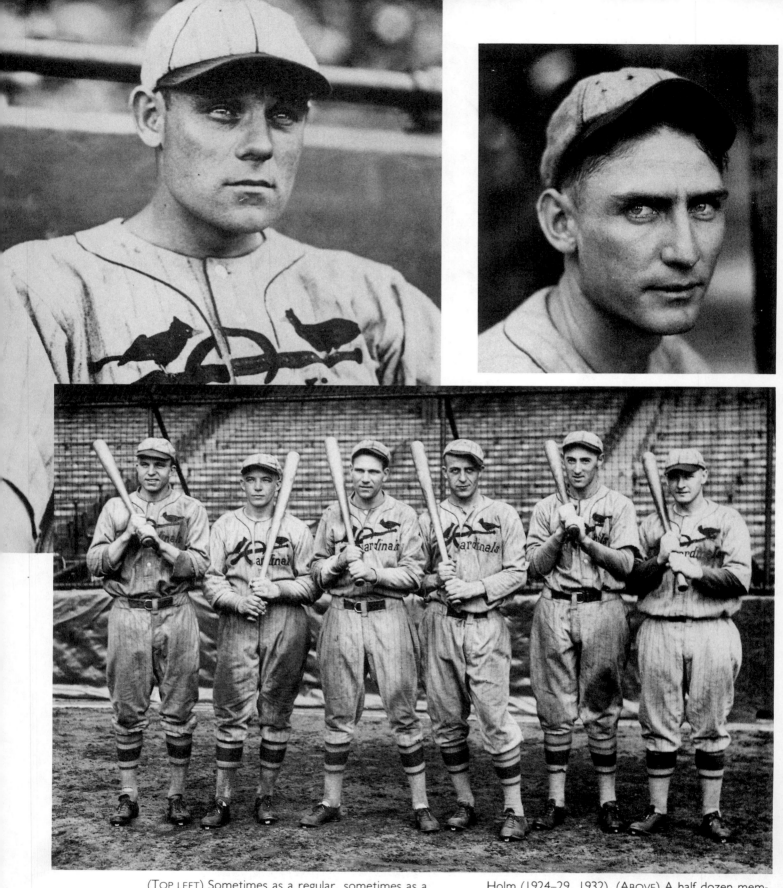

(TOP LEFT) Sometimes as a regular, sometimes as a reserve player, Ray Blades was in the Cardinal outfield from 1922 to 1932, with a .342 average in 1925 his best. Blades managed the Cards in 1939 and 1940. (TOP RIGHT) Reserve outfielder Wattie Holm (1924–29, 1932). (ABOVE) A half dozen members of the 1926 National League pennant winners. *Left to right:* Taylor Douthit, Billy Southworth, Les Bell, Jim Bottomley, Chick Hafey, and Bob O'Farrell.

Joe McCarthy took over the Chicago Cubs as manager that spring, he quickly lost patience with the genial but often erratic and unpredictable Alexander.

"Alex could still pitch," McCarthy said, "but he insisted on going by his own rules and that wasn't very good for the rest of the team. So I had to let him go."

With Alexander contributing nine victories, right-hander Flint Rhem fastballing himself to a 20-7 record, and Sherdel and Haines pitching winning ball, the Cardinals began moving up through the standings, battling doggedly with Cincinnati, Pittsburgh, and Chicago. The Cardinals whipped the Pirates in a double-header on August 31 and went into September in first place, faced with an unfortunate scheduling oddity—their entire September schedule was on the road.

For two weeks the Cardinals bobbed in and out of first place, then went into Philadelphia for a six-game series with the last-place Phillies.

"It was like an oasis for us," Les Bell remembered. "We'd just had some tough series in Cincinnati, Pittsburgh, and Boston, and we just plowed through the Phillies."

Hornsby's men took five out of six from the Phillies, edged into first place, and this time stayed there. On September 24, St. Louis clinched the pennant at the Polo Grounds when they defeated the Giants, 6–4. The final margin was two games over the Reds. Their 89 wins were the lowest for a National League pennant winner, up to that point.

For the city of St. Louis, it was the first championship since Chris Von Der Ahe's Browns had finished on top in the old American Association in 1888. Accordingly, the city broke into a celebration which newspapers compared to the municipal binge which marked the Armistice of November 11, 1918.

An early-season collision at second base had dislodged several vertebrae in Hornsby's back and interfered with his swing all summer, holding the skipper to an uncharacteristic .317 batting average. The team's top hitter was Bell (.325), followed by Hornsby, Southworth (.317 as a Cardinal), Douthit (.308), outfielder Ray

Bob O'Farrell (1925–28, 1933, 1935), who managed the Cardinals in 1927.

Blades (.305), and O'Farrell (.293). Bottomley hit .299 and led the league with 120 RBIs and 40 doubles. Hafey, playing just half the season, batted .271. The team's 90 home runs were the most in the league.

Rhem's 20 wins tied him for the league lead; no other Cardinal pitcher ranked high in any significant category. The club received a financial break when Phil Ball, expecting his Browns to contend for the pennant, expanded Sportsman's Park's seating capacity from 18,000 to 34,000. The benefit was reaped by Breadon, whose Redbirds drew a new team record 668,428, while the Browns, who disappeared into seventh place, pulled under 300,000.

Awaiting the Cardinals in the World Series were the New York Yankees, the team of Babe Ruth, Lou Gehrig (completing his second full year), Earle Combs, Bob Meusel, and rookie Tony Lazzeri—one of the most lethal lineups ever banded together. New York also had a well-stocked pitching staff in Waite Hoyt, Urban Shocker, Bob Shawkey, and left-handers

Billy Southworth coming home after hitting a homer in the seventh inning of Game 2 of the '26 World Series at Yankee Stadium.

Herb Pennock and Dutch Ruether. And, given the often ironic byways of baseball, managing the Yankees was former Cardinal skipper Miller Huggins, having just won his fourth pennant in six years.

The Series opened in New York, with Sherdel on the mound for the Cardinals against Pennock. The duel of left-handers was won by Pennock and the heavily favored Yankees, 2–1. St. Louis evened it the next day behind a masterful performance by Alexander. After falling behind 2–0 in the second inning, Alex settled down and began displaying the form that had earned him his own special pew in the history of pitching. Snapping off his sharp-breaking curves with immaculate precision, he retired the last 21 batters he faced. While Alex was shutting down the Yankee power plant, his teammates were pecking away at Shocker. In the top of the seventh, Southworth broke a 2–2 tie with a three-run homer. Shortstop Tommy Thevenow also homered for the Cardinals, who came away with a 6–2 win.

The Series then moved to St. Louis. For the Cardinals, who had been on the road since the beginning of September, this was their triumphant homecoming, and in honor of their heroes' return the city again turned on the emotional faucets and, as Frederick Lieb noted in his splendid history of the Cardinals, the front page of the *St. Louis Globe-Democrat* included these resounding headlines: "Tumultuous Thousands Welcome Cardinals," and "Greatest Demonstration in City's Baseball History as Frenzied Multitudes Lionize Baseball Heroes Amid Bedlam of Noise and Joyous Enthusiasm." The outpouring occurred during an open-car, ticker-tape parade.

"Remember now," Les Bell said, "this was right in the middle of things. I asked Sherdel what would happen if we won the Series."

" 'The whole city is going to jump into the Mississippi,' he said."

The Cardinals took Game 3 behind a 4–0 shutout by Haines (who also hit a home run). The Yankees evened it the next day, 10–5, with Ruth putting on the kind of show that in succeeding generations would be called "Ruthian." The Yankee slugger helped bury Flint Rhem and the Cardinals with three home runs. The Yankees then took Game 5, 3–2, Pennock again beating Sherdel, and the teams headed back to New York, where the general assumption was the Cardinals were cooked.

In Game 6, however, Alexander tied the Series with an easy 10–2 victory over Bob Shawkey, creating the last tomorrow.

Haines started the finale against Hoyt. In the bottom of the seventh inning the Cardinals were leading 3–2. The Yankees loaded the bases with two out and had rookie Tony Lazzeri at the plate. Haines, who threw his knuckler off the knuckles of his right hand, had been bearing down so hard that he had by now broken the skin on one finger and was bleeding. Hornsby removed him and called Alexander in from the bullpen.

The forty-year-old veteran had pitched nine innings the day before; nevertheless, with the team facing the season's critical moment, not even Rogers Hornsby could resist the allure of Grover Cleveland Alexander. There were younger and stronger pitchers available to him, but the skipper wanted Alex.

The moment has come down to us wreathed in mists of legend: Alexander had been drinking the night before and been sleeping in the bullpen when the call came; Hornsby walked out to short left field to meet him, to see if the old boy's eyes were clear; Alexander was hung over.

"None of that was true," said Les Bell, the third baseman. "Alex had had a few drinks the night before, but he wasn't drunk, because Rog had told him he might need Alex the next day. Alex wasn't sleeping in the pen and Rog didn't walk out to meet him. And Alex wasn't hung over—he stood there and told us exactly how he was going to pitch Lazzeri and his mind was sharp as a tack."

The plan was to tempt Lazzeri with an inside fastball, which Tony would pull foul; and then Alex would throw unhittable curves low and away.

Flint Rhem warming up for his Game 4 start in the 1926 World Series.

This is exactly what happened. Lazzeri pulled the fastball foul, then went down swinging on two sharp, back-breaking curve balls, just as Alexander the craftsman supreme had planned. The tense confrontation had more than drama in it, it also had romance and symbolism: the hard-hitting Lazzeri was a rookie—one writer described Tony as "pawing nervously at the dirt with his toe" and then "taking muscular practice swings" as he waited for Alexander to complete a long, deliberately slow walk from the bullpen to the mound. For Alexander, battered by alcoholism and epilepsy, his spirit shattered and tormented by World

Babe Ruth has just branded one of Rhem's pitches in the first inning of Game 4. Flint is on the mound watching it fly, as are catcher O'Farrell, umpire Bill Klem, and Mr. Ruth. It was the first of three home runs Ruth tagged that day.

War cannon fire, it was the theft of a moment from time just as his career had begun to slide over the horizon.

But after the crucial strikeout, Alex still had two more innings to go. He got through the eighth without blemish, then retired the first two men in the bottom of the ninth, and came to Ruth, who in a one-run game was pure menace.

"I wasn't going to let that big monkey tie me," Alex said later.

Pitching carefully to Ruth, who had already hit all four Yankee home runs in the Series, Alex walked him. With Alexander pitching to Bob Meusel, Ruth, in what has been described as "the only mistake he ever made on a baseball diamond," inexplicably tried to steal second base. O'Farrell's on-the-money peg to Hornsby shot down the great man and the Cardinals were world champions.

St. Louis's baseball euphoria lasted for just two months; to be precise, until December 20.

Grover Cleveland Alexander *(left)* and Bob Shawkey, starting pitchers for Game 6 of the 1926 World Series.

A couple of monumental talents doing the traditional thing at the '26 World Series. Babe Ruth *(left)* and Rogers Hornsby.

Trouble had arisen in September, when Hornsby asked Breadon to cancel an exhibition game in New Haven that Sam had scheduled early in the season. With the Cardinals coming down the stretch in a grueling pennant race, the skipper preferred that his boys have the day off. Breadon tried to cancel the game but was unable to. When Hornsby heard this he was furious. Rogers, who led the league in everything but tact, accused Breadon of being more interested in picking up a few dollars than in winning the pennant.

It was a monumental clashing of strong personalities. Breadon was as tough and as sharp-tongued as his star. (There had been other disputes between the two: Hornsby had once even ordered Sam out of the clubhouse, in front of the whole team. In addition, Hornsby was asking for a three-year contract at $50,000 per year, enough to elevate the penurious Breadon's eyebrows and freeze them there.) These two hard-nosed, stubborn men were, in many respects, evenly matched. In one crucial respect, they were not: Breadon owned the team.

Star players had been traded before, and have since, but never one who was freshly arrived at a pinnacle achievement, as Hornsby was in 1926. Rogers straddled St. Louis like a colossus. Newspapers were featuring him in articles, advertisers were begging him for endorsements, women were sending him perfumed handkerchiefs in the mail. And then suddenly he was gone. It was as if Breadon had punctured the fantasies and struck at the pride of every Cardinal fan. Black crepe was hung over the doors of Sam's home and at his automobile agency. He had to disconnect his telephone to spare himself torrents of frenzied abuse. Civic groups organized and threatened to boycott the team. Sam was denounced in newspaper editorials that rang with outrage and indignation.

Hornsby still held stock in the Cardinals and before he could play for the Giants this had to be bought up. It took the personal intervention of league president John Heydler to bring the matter to a conclusion, and when it was finally done—shortly before the opening of the 1927 season—the shrewd Hornsby was paid

Rogers Hornsby facing the latest thing in studio microphones.

That was the day the people of St. Louis walked up to each other and said, "Have you heard?" and "Do you believe it?" Provoking the incredulity was this: Rogers Hornsby had been traded to the New York Giants.

Those who were privy to the backstage tension that had existed between Breadon and Hornsby weren't entirely surprised by the trade.

Frankie Frisch (1927–37, manager 1933–38). "The Fordham Flash" batted over .300 seven times for the Redbirds.

$116,000 for the stock he had paid $50,000 for just two years before. Even by the heady standards of the Roaring Twenties, this was quite a profit.

And who could the Cardinals possibly receive in return for the league's premier hitter? Well, they got a man who, in all-around ability, was a match for just about anybody who ever played the game: Frankie Frisch.

The twenty-eight-year-old Frisch had joined the Giants out of Fordham University (hence his nickname, "The Fordham Flash") in 1919 and, playing second base and third, became a star of John McGraw's 1921–24 pennant winners. While not a hitter of Hornsby's caliber (his highest average was .348), Frisch was a dynamo on the field, hard-driving, swift afoot, and fiercely competitive. A natural leader, he was intelligent, sharp-tongued, and a hard loser. Given his zealous spirit, it was inevitable he would clash with the abusive, dictatorial McGraw.

Left to right: Shortstop Charley Gelbert (1929–32, 1935–36), Billy Southworth, and Frankie Frisch in 1929.

A gaggle of Cardinals. *Left to right:* Les Bell, Bob O'Farrell, Jim Bottomley, and Billy Southworth.

While McGraw never had a player he admired more than Frisch, the personal conflicts and collisions between the two men had developed into a festering mutual hatred. McGraw seemed to go out of his way to criticize and insult his star player, and Frisch would not take it, answering back in kind, which none of his players had ever done to the imperious John J. McGraw. Finally, late in the 1926 season, Frisch had had a bellyful and abruptly jumped the team for several days. McGraw never forgave him. So when both the Cardinals and Giants had an opportunity to rid themselves of their "problem" players, the trade was made. Along with Frisch to St. Louis came right-

hander Jimmy Ring, once a fine pitcher but now on the down side.

St. Louis fans were, understandably, cool to Frisch in the beginning, but Frankie's aggressive style of play soon won them over. As St. Louis sportswriter Bob Broeg put it, Frisch didn't make them forget Hornsby—he made them remember Frisch. (And Breadon, who had been alarmed at the hostility and vituperation aimed at him in the wake of the deal, was forever grateful to Frisch, saying that "Frank made it possible for me to remain in St. Louis.")

The new manager was Bob O'Farrell, and the strong-armed catcher came close to leading the club to a second straight pennant. At the end, though, the Cardinals finished 1½ games behind Pittsburgh. Otherwise, it was a hugely successful season—the team won 92 games,

Shortstop Tommy Thevenow (1924–28), a modest hitter who caught fire in the 1926 World Series with ten hits and a .417 average.

The new skipper was Bill McKechnie, who had won a pennant with the Pirates in 1925. "Deacon" Bill was a wise, soft-spoken, highly regarded baseball man who played a conservative brand of ball.

McKechnie's steady hand guided the Cardinals through another blistering pennant race in 1928, and this time St. Louis came out on top, winning a team-high 95 games, two ahead of the Giants. The summer's long excitement generated yet another club attendance record of 761,574, which was to remain the standard until 1946.

Jesse Haines, who won 24 games for the Cardinals in 1927.

more than any other Cardinal team ever had, and set a new attendance record of 749,340.

The Cardinals probably would have won the pennant in 1927 if they had not lost shortstop Tommy Thevenow to a broken leg in June and had O'Farrell not been limited to 61 games because of a sore arm. Frisch, however, batted .337, led the league with 48 stolen bases, and dazzled the fans with his hustle and sharp glovework around second base. (He set still-current records for second basemen with 641 assists and 1,037 chances.) Haines had his best year on the mound (24–10), while the forty-one-year-old Alexander was 21–10.

Despite his successful season, O'Farrell was relieved of his managerial duties by Breadon, who did not feel that Bob possessed the needed leadership qualities. (O'Farrell was retained as a player, but early in the 1928 season was traded to the Giants.)

Manager Bill McKechnie (left) and Grover Cleveland Alexander in 1928.

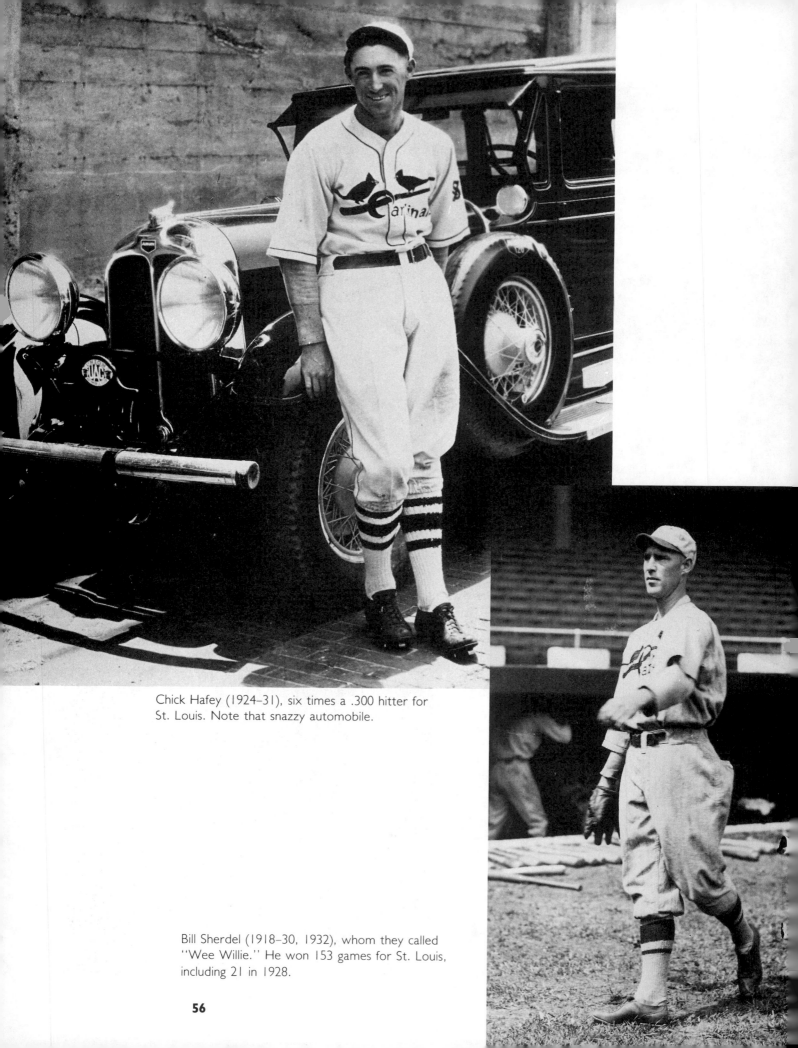

Chick Hafey (1924–31), six times a .300 hitter for
St. Louis. Note that snazzy automobile.

Bill Sherdel (1918–30, 1932), whom they called
"Wee Willie." He won 153 games for St. Louis,
including 21 in 1928.

With the exception of four days in late August, the Cardinals held the lead from June 15 to the end, clinching the day before the season ended. Bottomley was the club's big hitter, batting .325 and leading the league in home runs (31) and RBIs (136). Hafey bloomed to stardom with a .337 average and 111 RBIs, and Frisch batted an even .300. George Harper, an outfielder acquired from the Giants in exchange for O'Farrell, batted .305 and on September 20 became the first Cardinal to hit three home runs in a game. On May 11, the club made another key acquisition when they obtained catcher Jimmie Wilson from the Phillies for catcher Spud Davis and outfielder Homer Peel. Wilson, whose nickname was "Ace," was an outstanding defensive catcher.

Haines (20–8) had his last big year, while Sherdel was 21–10 and Alexander 16–9.

St. Louis's opposition in the World Series once again were Miller Huggins' Yankees. Having beaten this great team two years before, the Cardinals entered the October festivity brimming with confidence, especially with New York's left-handed ace Herb Pennock out with a sore arm and center fielder Earle Combs sidelined with a broken finger. So it was a stunned Cardinal team that found itself steamrolled in four by the Yankees. There was nothing McKechnie's pitchers could do to stop Ruth and Gehrig. Babe batted .625 and hit three home runs, all in the fourth game; Gehrig batted .545, hit four homers, and drove in nine runs.

Huggins used just three pitchers to win the championship. Waite Hoyt won the opener and the finale by scores of 4–1 and 7–3, George Pipgras took Game 2, 9–3, and lefty Tom Zachary Game 3, 7–3.

The World Series debacle so angered Brea-

Action in the 1928 World Series. It's the top of the second inning of Game 2 at Yankee Stadium. The Yankees are in the midst of making a double play. Shortstop Mark Koenig has just fed to second baseman Tony Lazzeri, who is about to fire on to Lou Gehrig. The baserunner is Alexander.

Center fielder Taylor Douthit (1923–31), solid man on three Cardinal pennant winners. He had more than 200 hits in 1929 and 1930.

His name was High, but he stood only 5′6″. That's Andy High, who gave the Cards some good innings at third base from 1928 to 1931.

Veteran southpaw Clarence Mitchell (1928–30). It was Mitchell, with Brooklyn in 1920, who lined into the only unassisted triple play in World Series history.

in the first inning and ten more in the fifth.) In this game, Hafey began a string of ten consecutive hits, tying a league record.

After 88 games, Breadon again switched managers, bringing McKechnie back to St. Louis and returning Southworth to Rochester. Neither manager was able to get the club moving and the defending league champions finished fourth. The team batted .293, with five men at .325 or more, but this was one of the loudest hitting seasons in league history (the loudest of all was coming up in 1930) and the Cardinals were outhit by four other teams.

As the season was winding down, it took into its vortex the sad finale of Grover Cleveland Alexander. After going on the wagon for a while, the now forty-two-year-old legend showed up one day in New York trembling

Nearing the end of the line, Grover Cleveland Alexander is caught in a moment of contemplation.

Right-hander Sylvester Johnson (1926–33). He was 13–7 in 1929, his top year.

don that he demoted his pennant-winning manager to Rochester and hired that club's skipper, Billy Southworth, to run the Cardinals in 1929.

Southworth got the team off to a good start—the Redbirds were hovering around the top of the league in mid-June—but then the walls caved in. A ten-game losing streak put the team into a spin from which they never seemed to recover, though the breaking of the streak was a resounding event: on July 6, the Cardinals got back into the victory column with a 28–6 mashing of the Phillies at Philadelphia's Baker Bowl, a run total that remains the National League record. (The Cardinals scored ten runs

A straw-hatted crowd lining up outside Sportsman's Park on a summer's day in the 1920s.

and disheveled. Sobriety had proven an unmanageable burden. When McKechnie put him in to pitch two days later, Alex was hit hard. McKechnie had no choice but to send Alexander back to St. Louis. Breaden, always partial to the man who had saved the 1926 World Series, paid him off in full and sent him home to Nebraska.

"He was very sad and apologetic," Breadon said later. "He told me that drink had been a weakness in his family and that it had been too much for him."

In December, Alexander was dealt to the Phillies, for whom he had enjoyed his greatest success in the years before World War I. Alex was beyond winning now, and after going 0–4 was released. He ended his career with 373 victories, the same as Christy Mathewson, and they remain at the top of the National League win list. If he had not stumbled and fallen off the wagon and missed the last six weeks of the 1929 season, Alex would in all probability have surpassed Mathewson and become the National League's all-time winning pitcher.

PEPPER, DIZZY, AND THE GANG

WHEN BILL McKECHNIE was offered a long-term contract to manage the Boston Braves, Breadon gave him permission to take it. There was reason for McKechnie to find the security appealing, for with his departure the Cardinals were starting a sixth straight season with a sixth different manager—Rickey in 1925, Hornsby in 1926, O'Farrell in 1927, McKechnie in 1928, Southworth in 1929, and now in 1930 Charles ("Gabby") Street.

Street, a forty-seven-year-old Alabaman, had caught for the Reds, Braves, Senators, and Yankees between 1904 and 1912. He had been known as an able catcher, a weak hitter (.208 lifetime), and for having caught a ball dropped from the Washington Monument as a publicity stunt.

Along with his "Gabby" nickname, Street was also known as "Sarge" for his service in the World War, during which he had seen some pretty hot action in the Argonne. In the National League in 1930 he would see the big guns roaring again, baseball style. With the ball at its liveliest, the league went on a summer-long hitting binge that left the record book as well as the psyches of a lot of pitchers in tatters. So many offensive records were set in 1930 that some thought should be given to using asterisks for that year. Thanks to a hyperactive ball, the league batted .303, with six teams averaging over .300 (the Giants topped off at an all-timer high .319 club mark).

The Cardinals swung away for a .314 team average, with every regular checking in at over .300: Bottomley .304, Frisch .346, shortstop Charley Gelbert .304, third baseman Sparky Adams .314, Wilson .318, and outfielders Douthit .303, Hafey .336, and rookie George Watkins .373, which set the all-time major

Gabby Street, Cardinal manager from 1929 to 1933.

Jim Bottomley, who lost the batting title by an eyelash to teammate Chick Hafey in 1931.

Earl ("Sparky") Adams (1930–33). The third baseman batted .314 in 1930 as part of St. Louis's all-.300-hitting lineup.

league record for freshmen. In addition, outfielder Showboat Fisher batted .374 in 92 games and catcher Gus Mancuso .366 for 76 games. The team rapped a major league record 373 doubles (Frisch was the team leader with 46), scored 1,004 runs—still the league's highest—and had a club record 1,732 hits.

Street's top pitcher was hard-throwing left-hander Bill Hallahan, known as "Wild Bill" because he was once photographed sitting astride a horse (he also led in walks three times). A farm system product, Bill was 15–9 and the league's strikeout leader with 177. Veteran spitballer Burleigh Grimes, acquired in a June trade with the Braves (for Sherdel and right-hander Fred Frankhouse), was 13–6 for St. Louis, while Haines was 13–8 and Rhem and Sylvester Johnson each won 12.

Charley Gelbert. A hunting accident in 1932 wrecked his career.

Gus Mancuso (1928–32, 1941–42), one of the fine catchers of his time.

This club gave Street a pennant-winner in his first year as manager, edging the Cubs by two games. It was the Cardinals' third pennant in five years, each under a different manager.

The pennant winners didn't do it by playing consistent ball. In last place on May 6, they suddenly became inspired and took 17 of 18, then went into immediate reverse and dropped 12 of 13. On August 8 they trailed first-place Brooklyn by 12 games, but then found the right elixir again and went on to win 39 of their last 49 and squeezed through to their two-game margin at season's end.

St. Louis's left-handed ace Bill Hallahan (1925–26, 1929–36). He shut out great Philadelphia Athletic teams in both the 1930 and 1931 World Series.

Frankie Frisch ripping one in spring training.

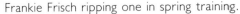

A key, mid-September series in Brooklyn produced one of baseball's all-time fantastic tales, concerning Flint Rhem. A talented pitcher with a big league thirst for Prohibition booze,

Flint had been sent to the minors in the hope the demotion would sober him up. Now he was back and pitching well. Penciled in to work the opener against the Dodgers, Flint wandered into the hotel that morning with his eyes swimming, his clothing disheveled, his hand unsteady. The tale he had to tell was a beauty. Two men, it seemed, had kidnapped him the night before, driven him to a house in New Jersey, and by gunpoint forced him to drink cup after cup of straight whisky. They were gamblers, Flint averred, who were plunging heavily on Brooklyn the next day and wanted to turn him into a wet rag so he wouldn't be able to pitch.

The thought of someone forcing Flint to drink whisky against his will was as fanciful as ordering the ocean tides to go somewhere they didn't want to. While no one believed Flint, no one ever disproved his story either. As one teammate said, "Anybody who tried to investigate that story to see if it was true or not was out of his mind."

Flint Rhem, who claimed he was forced to drink whisky at gunpoint on the eve of a key game during the Cardinals' stretch drive in 1930.

A jubilant St. Louis greeting its pennant winners in a victory parade on September 27, 1930. Gabby Street (in hat) and Frankie Frisch are in the lead car.

So Rhem was scratched and Hallahan started. (An amused Hallahan lifted the blinds on Flint's story years later, telling a writer that "some friends of Flint's had come up from South Carolina to see the games in New York and Brooklyn. After the games in the Polo Grounds they went out for a few drinks and just kept going.")

Hallahan had problems of his own. The day before, a taxi door had slammed shut on his right hand, leaving him in considerable pain. When Street asked if he could pitch, the gutty Hallahan said, "I pitch with my left hand." Then he went out and delivered what he called the game of his life, shutting out Brooklyn and the great Dazzy Vance 1–0 in ten innings. From there the Cardinals charged on to their third pennant.

On the last day of the season, the Cardinals began a new chapter in their history. With the pennant having already been iced, Street gave

the ball to a tall, lanky nineteen-year-old with an ingratiating personality, a radiant self-confidence, a mile-wide grin, and a smoking fastball. This was Dizzy Dean (he variously gave his first name as Jerome or Jay), who had pitched at St. Joseph in the Western Association and Houston in the Texas League and rung

Burleigh Grimes (*right*) greeting Commissioner Kenesaw Mountain Landis at the 1930 World Series.

It's a bang-bang play at second as Frisch nails Philadelphia's Mickey Cochrane trying to steal. Shortstop Charley Gelbert is watching the action as umpire Cy Rigler makes the call. The play occurred in the first inning of Game I of the 1930 World Series.

up a combined 25–10 record. In his debut performance the youngster three-hit the Pirates, 3–1.

If the Yankee clubs St. Louis had faced in the 1926 and 1928 World Series were among the greatest ever, so were the Cards' opponents in 1930, Connie Mack's Philadelphia Athletics, who were in the midst of three straight pennants. The A's were built around catcher Mickey Cochrane, first baseman Jimmie Foxx, outfielder Al Simmons, and pitchers Lefty Grove and George Earnshaw.

The Series opened in Philadelphia, with Grove beating Grimes, 5–2. Burleigh yielded only five hits, but all were for extra bases and each produced a run. The next day Earnshaw whipped Rhem, 6–1.

When the pageant moved to St. Louis, Hallahan shut out the mighty A's in Game 3, 5–0. The Cardinals tied it the next day on a Haines four-hitter, beating Grove, 3–1. Game 5 proved to be pivotal. Grimes dueled Earnshaw and then Grove, who relieved in the eighth, to a scoreless tie into the top of the ninth. Then Burleigh walked Cochrane and was tagged by a resounding Foxx home run. Remembering the blow years later, Grimes said, "He hit it so hard I couldn't feel sorry for myself."

The following day the Athletics disposed of Hallahan early and, behind Earnshaw, who was pitching on one day's rest, rolled to a 7–1 victory and the world championship.

Slightly embarrassed by the barrage of base hits in 1930, and faced with players demanding higher salaries commensurate with their higher averages, the owners deactivated the ball the following year and as a consequence the National League batting average dropped from .303 to a more seemly .277.

After having had to grind out their previous pennants in lockstep races, the Cardinals surprised everyone by running off with an easy victory in 1931, winning 101 games (a new team record) and taking the banner by 13 games. This was the year the Baseball Writers of America Association began selecting Most Valuable Players and the first winner in the Na-

tional League was Frisch, who batted .311, led the league with 28 stolen bases, and galvanized the team with his blazing play.

While Frisch was earning the MVP Award, Hafey was winning the closest batting race in big league history—.3489 to .3486 for New

Outfielder George Watkins (1930–33), who set a rookie record with his .373 batting average in 1930 but never came close to that again.

Branch Rickey, architect of the vaunted St. Louis farm system.

York's Bill Terry and .3482 for Chick's team-mate Jim Bottomley. Watkins dropped from his rookie record .373 to .288, a victim of the more pacified baseball.

With the farm system becoming more and more productive, Rickey was able to indulge

Pepper Martin (1928, 1930–40, 1944). He batted .418 in two World Series.

Right-hander Paul Derringer (1931–33), who was 18-8 as a rookie in 1931.

what was going to become a familiar penchant—selling off older, still productive stars and replacing them with younger players, who commanded smaller salaries. In June, Rickey dealt Taylor Douthit (batting .331 at the time) to Cincinnati and installed Johnny Leonard Roosevelt ("Pepper") Martin in center field.

Martin, who batted .300 in his first full year, was an aggressive, hard-playing, and very likable Oklahoman. Pepper's style of play was as uninhibited as his mischievous personality; his bristling presence on the field can best be summed up in the words of a National League infielder: "Once we had three guys chasing him around in a run-down and *we* were the ones who felt surrounded."

Hallahan was 19–9, leading the league in wins (it was the first time in its history that the National League was without a twenty-game winner) and strikeouts (159). Right behind Bill was rookie right-hander Paul Derringer (18–8), Grimes (17–9), and Haines, who coaxed a 12–3 record out of his thirty-seven-year-old arm.

For the second straight year Connie Mack's juggernaut Philadelphia Athletics were sharing the World Series stage with the Cardinals. But this time the Cardinals had, in Hallahan's words, "a secret weapon named Pepper Martin."

The 1931 World Series has gone down in history as "The Pepper Martin Series." For one week in October Pepper ran wild and helped dispel the country's Depression blues. The hawk-nosed Oklahoma rookie with the bubbling energy, whom Rickey once called "one of nature's noblemen," bedeviled the powerful A's throughout the Series, particularly during the first five games.

The A's won the opener, 6–2, Grove (a 31-game winner that year) beating Derringer, despite Martin's two singles, double, and stolen base. Hallahan evened it the next day with a 2–0, three-hit shutout. Martin doubled, stole third, and scored the first run, then singled, stole second, and eventually scored the second run on a squeeze bunt.

Grimes beat Grove in Game 3, 5–2, with

Getting together at the 1931 World Series are *(left to right)*, Jim Bottomley,
Pepper Martin, Chick Hafey, Al Simmons, and Mickey Cochrane.

Pepper building his legend during the '31 Series. The catcher is Mickey Cochrane.

Pepper contributing a single and double and scoring two runs. Earnshaw then evened the Series with a 3–0, two-hit blanker, Pepper collecting both hits. In Game 5, Martin (now elevated to the clean-up spot by Street) whacked two singles and a home run and drove in four runs in Hallahan's 5–1 victory.

Pepper was now 12-for-18 in the Series. He did not hit safely in Game 6 as Grove beat Derringer 8–1, nor in the finale, in which Grimes, with last-out help from Hallahan, gave the Cardinals the championship with a 4–2 win. Burleigh had taken a 4–0 lead into the top of the ninth, but the A's scored twice and had the tying runs on base when Hallahan came in and got the final out—on a fly ball, lifted, appropriately enough, to St. Louis's "secret weapon" in center field, Pepper Martin.

Pepper ended the Series with 12 hits and a .500 batting average. He had one home run, four doubles, five RBIs, five runs scored, and five stolen bases. After the Series, Commissioner Kenesaw Mountain Landis congratulated the exuberant Martin and said, "Young man, I'd rather trade places with you than with any man in the country," to which Pepper replied, "Fine, Judge, if we can swap salaries, too." (Landis was making $60,000 to Pepper's $4,500. It gave Martin a permanent entry in baseball's book of famous quotes.)

In the off-season the Cardinals unloaded Grimes and his high salary ($20,000, along with Frisch's tops on the club) to the Cubs for pitcher Bud Teachout and one-time home run champ Hack Wilson. (In January, the canny Rickey sold Wilson to Brooklyn for $45,000.) Then, just before the opening of the 1932 season, the club dealt its batting champion Chick Hafey to Cincinnati, in return getting two players and a sizable check. Hafey had been holding out for more money, and in those days this was as good as a ticket out of St. Louis. While Cardinal fans did some grumbling over the deals, Grimes was in fact just about finished as a winning pitcher and the Cardinal farm system, operating on all cylinders, was able to replace even a player of Hafey's stature.

Pepper Martin bedeviling Mickey Cochrane in the '31 Series, scoring on a squeeze play during the seventh inning of Game 2. The umpire is Dick Nallin.

Chick Hafey won the batting crown in 1931 and then was traded.

Dizzy Dean (1930, 1932–37).

The world champions never quite gelled in 1932 and dropped through the league to a tie for sixth place. The season was notable, however, for the arrival of the man who was to become the most famous Cardinal of them all—Dizzy Dean.

After his impressive debut in the last game of 1930, Dean assumed he would be on the staff in 1931. But the youngster's cocky, outspoken self-confidence so annoyed Street that the skipper (with Rickey's concurrence) decided to send him back to the minors for another year. Dizzy toured the Texas League like a tornado, posting a 26–10 record and ringing up 303 strikeouts, and in 1932 there was no question about him making the team. Now all of twenty-one years old, the rookie, who talked almost as fast as he threw, was 18–15 and the strikeout leader with 191.

In a few years the Arkansas-born right-hander was to replace a fading Babe Ruth as baseball's premier name and gate attraction as he enjoyed one of the game's merriest albeit sadly aborted careers.

Dean was an original, a character that Mark Twain or Ring Lardner might have conjured. Sprung from a background of rural poverty and hardship, Dean never lost his sense of humor, his gusto approach to life, nor his ability to charm those around him. He was a refreshing gale of optimism in those bleak, flat, and sour Depression years.

With all his other charms and talents, Dean was a sly manipulator of the press. Realizing that he was perceived as a prime slice of American hayseed, Dizzy played the role shrewdly, delighting the representatives of urban journalism with corn-fed wisecracks, stories, and postures. "He played his tunes right across the backs of the city slickers," one writer said, and they loved it. He suggested to the press that they call him "The Great One," and, as another writer said, "He was ingenuous enough not to seem arrogant, and he was good enough to back it up." It was this latter, of course, which made Dizzy Dean significant: a live fastball, a big, sharp curve, and a change-up which he mixed deftly with his hard stuff.

Joe ("Ducky") Medwick (1932–40, 1947–48). After Rogers Hornsby and before Stan Musial, he was the Cardinals' top hitter.

At the end of the 1932 season the Cardinals broke another talented youngster into the lineup, Joe Medwick. The twenty-year-old left fielder out of Carteret, New Jersey, would become second only to Hornsby among all-time Cardinal right-handed hitters. Possessing one of the fiercest line-drive bats ever seen in baseball, Joe was known as a "bad-ball hitter," swinging at anything he liked, and off the field swinging at anything he disliked. They called him "Muscles," which tells you something; they also called him "Ducky," for a somewhat waddling way of walking. He could be surly, short-tempered; once he even decked the great Dean in the dugout when Dizzy had the temerity to question Joe's hustle in left field. Joe was as subtle as the line drives he whacked to all fields, but he became the National League's top hitter of the 1930s. In 26 tail-end games in 1932, Joe gave St. Louis fans a glimpse into the future by ringing up league pitching for a .349 average.

Left to right: Dizzy Dean, Branch Rickey, and Frankie Frisch sharing a laugh in spring training.

An off-season misfortune cost the club their regular shortstop. In mid-November, Charley Gelbert was tramping the autumn woods near McConnellsburg, Pennsylvania, in search of small game. His foot caught in the undergrowth and he stumbled, and in so doing his rifle discharged, the full charge tearing into his left leg. It would be 1935 before Gelbert returned to the major leagues. Only twenty-six years old at the time of the accident, he was never the same player after it. He was a utility infielder with the Cardinals in 1935 and 1936, then was traded.

Having lost his regular shortstop, Rickey was pressed to replace him. The price was steep. The man Rickey wanted was Cincinnati's Leo Durocher, light of stick but brilliant afield. It was a six-player deal, with Leo and two nondescript pitchers going to St. Louis in exchange for Paul Derringer, Allyn Stout, and Sparky Adams. With Derringer going on to become one of the great pitchers of his time with the Reds, the deal was called one of Rickey's few trading mistakes; but the Cardinals needed a

shortstop and the short-term dividends of the trade were clearly in St. Louis's favor.

The twenty-seven-year-old Durocher would spend another forty years in baseball, as player, coach, broadcaster, and, most prominently, as manager of the Brooklyn Dodgers, New York Giants, Chicago Cubs, and Houston Astros. He remains one of baseball's all-time controversial characters. Along with possessing one of the game's keenest minds, Leo was loud of voice, sharp of tongue, and provocative. Few men in the game's history ever had as many devoted admirers or as many sworn enemies as the man who came to be known as "The Lip."

Along with the agitating Durocher, the Cards also had the irascible Medwick, the ebullient Dean, the irrepressible Martin, the dynamic Frisch, and the fun-loving first baseman Rip Collins, who had replaced Bottomley. If the Cardinals had gone out to handpick vivid and singular personalities, they couldn't have done better. The nucleus of "The Gashouse Gang," baseball's most raucous assemblage ever, was now in place.

Leo Durocher (1933–37). He could out-field any shortstop and out-talk anybody.

Rip Collins (1931–36). His 35 homers led the league in 1934.

The Cardinals finished fifth in 1933, but looked good doing it, with an 82–71 record, only 4½ games out of second place. In late July, Street was let out as manager and replaced by Frisch, who was the ideal leader for this club. Frankie was as tough as any of them, had as sharp a sense of humor, and with his shouts, threats, and low boiling point, was a sitting duck for Gashouse humor—Martin would drop water bombs on the skipper's head from hotel windows, Dean might hand him an exploding cigar, Collins might mimic Frankie's high-pitched ranting. "But," Dean said, "we liked and admired Frank. When a guy blew up as beautifully as Frank did, you had to play a joke on him now and then."

But nobody was laughing on July 2. This was the day when the Giants' exquisite left-hander Carl Hubbell turned in what some people still think is the greatest pitching effort in baseball history. Facing the Cardinals in the first game of a doubleheader at the Polo Grounds, the poker-faced Hubbell went all 18 innings in beating the Cardinals 1–0, allowing just six hits and no walks. Right-hander Tex Carleton (pitching on two days' rest) went the first 16 for St. Louis, then turned the ball over to Haines, who lost it in the 18th. In the second game, New York's Roy Parmelee beat Dean by the same 1–0 score, allowing four hits. So the St. Louis ledger for the day showed 27 innings played, ten hits, and no runs.

Dizzy had a better day on July 30, when he set a new major league record by striking out 17 Chicago Cubs. The young right-hander was a twenty-game winner for the first time in 1933, going 20–18 and leading the league in strikeouts (199) and complete games (26).

The first All-Star Game was played that year, on July 6, at Chicago's Comiskey Park, and the Cardinals had the distinction of having four players in the National League's starting lineup: catcher Jimmie Wilson, pitcher Bill Hallahan, second baseman Frankie Frisch, and Pepper Martin, who was now a third baseman.

The 1934 Cardinals remain one of baseball's unforgettable teams. Their hellbent style of play earned them their "Gashouse Gang" label; originally meant to be critical, it became the banner they sailed under because it seemed fitting and right, and the players came to be proud of it. Frisch's band of brawling, mischievous baseball delinquents fought Bill Terry's New York Giants through one of the league's hottest pennant races and won it on the season's final weekend.

The cast of characters included Dizzy Dean, at peak form that year with a 30–7 record, and his younger brother Paul, nicknamed "Daffy," though he was as reserved as Dizzy was gregarious, who was 19–11. (Dizzy had predicted they would win 45 between them. When he heard this rather grandiose forecast in the spring, the laconic Paul said, "That's right. I'll win ten and Diz can take care of the rest.") Rip Collins was at first base, batting .333, driving in 128 runs, and tying New York's Mel Ott for the home run lead with 35. The thirty-five-year-old Frisch played second and batted .305. Durocher was at short and Martin at third, as chattery a left side as any infield has ever had. Medwick was in left, batting .319 and driving

Catcher Jimmie Wilson (1928–33). Burleigh Grimes said Jimmie was the smartest catcher he ever had.

Dizzy Dean tuning up for what would be his 30-game season in 1934.

in 106 runs. Ernie Orsatti, a snazzy character who was a Hollywood agent in the off-season, was in center, batting .300. Former American Leaguer Jack Rothrock was in right. Catching were Spud Davis (.300) and young Bill De-Lancey (.316). Behind the Deans were Tex Carleton (16–11) and lefty Bill Walker (12–4).

Dizzy was, of course, the club's living logo. Tireless—he started 33 games and relieved in 17 others—he led in strikeouts for the third straight year (195) and shutouts (7). Paul, who some said fired harder than his big brother, had five shutouts. The brothers made news in August when they failed to show up for an exhibition game in Detroit and were fined, $100 for Dizzy, $50 for Paul, fines they said they would not pay. To emphasize their stand, Dizzy allowed himself to be photographed tearing up a pair of Cardinal uniforms. When the club stood its ground, the brothers backed down and what passed for normalcy among The Gashouse Gang returned.

Bill Terry's Giants, the 1933 world champions, were expected to repeat in 1934, and for much of the season the Giants looked solid. In mid-August the Cardinals were in third place, 7½ behind. On Labor Day, September 3, they were a little better off—five games out. On September 10 they were still five out. A week later they trailed by 3½. On September 21 Frisch took his gang into Brooklyn's Ebbets Field for a doubleheader, with the Deans scheduled to start. In the opener Dizzy won a 13–0 shutout and in the afterpiece Paul uncorked a 3–0 no-hitter. The club kept edging closer; on September 24 they were a mere 2½ behind New York.

On September 26, Dizzy pitched his team to a victory that put them just one game behind the Giants. Two days later the teams were tied for first place, with the season's final weekend at hand. The Giants had two games scheduled at the Polo Grounds with the Dodgers, while the Cardinals were at home for two with Cincinnati.

The Dodger-Giant games, emotion-packed at any time, were given a particular zest now because of a Bill Terry wisecrack early in the year. When asked about his intracity rival's chances, the usually humorless Terry tried a bit of wit: "Oh," he asked, "is Brooklyn still in the league?" So, with Terry's knee-slapper ringing in their ears, thousands of grudge-nursing Dodger fans rode the subway to upper Manhattan and packed the Polo Grounds to cheer their club into redeeming an otherwise dismal season by ruining the Giants' pennant chances.

On Saturday the Dodgers won, 5–1, while in St. Louis Paul Dean beat the Reds 6–1, putting the Cardinals a game up. On Sunday the Dodgers eliminated the Giants, while Dizzy, going on one day's rest, won his 30th on a 9–0 shutout, giving St. Louis a two-game edge at the end.

After having played the New York Yankees and Philadelphia Athletics in their previous four World Series appearances, the Cardinals found themselves up against another powerhouse opponent in the Detroit Tigers. Led by catcher-

Jim Lindsey (1929–34). He was an effective relief pitcher for the Redbirds.

Pepper Martin about to make a Gashouse Leap. Pittsburgh's great Pie Traynor is the third baseman, George Barr the umpire.

manager Mickey Cochrane, Detroit had won its first pennant in 25 years, sending the city on wheels into extremes of delight. (Cochrane had been sold from the Athletics to the Tigers by a cash-hungry Connie Mack.)

Along with Cochrane, the Tiger attack was led by first baseman Hank Greenberg, second baseman Charlie Gehringer, and outfielder Goose Goslin—the "G-Men"—along with shortstop Billy Rogell, third baseman Marv Owen, and outfielders Pete Fox, Jo-Jo White, and Gerald Walker. On the mound Cochrane had a formidable pair of 20-game winners in right-handers Tommy Bridges and Schoolboy Rowe, along with 15-game winners Eldon Auker and Fred Marberry. On paper, the Tigers were the stronger team. But as wise men have been known to say, the game is not played on paper but on grass. And anyway, that noted prognosticator Dizzy Dean had already announced

that "Me 'n Paul" would win two games apiece.

The Series opened in Detroit with Dizzy pointing the club in the right direction with an 8–3 win, Medwick out front with four hits. The Tigers evened it the next day, Rowe winning in 12 innings, 3–2.

The Cardinals won Game 3 behind Paul Dean, 4–1, but Detroit came right back the next day with a 10–4 win. It was in the fourth inning of this game that Dizzy Dean put on an unforgettable exhibition of baserunning. It occurred in the fourth inning. With the Tigers winning 3–1, the Cardinals began a rally. They had men on first and second when Spud Davis singled in a run. Frisch decided to pinch-run for the heavy-legged Davis and was looking up and down the bench when Dean, on his own, ran out to first base.

"Frisch frowned when he saw Dizzy out there," Bill Hallahan said. "He didn't like the idea. You don't put 30-game winners in as pinch-runners. But the guy was already on the field, so he said, 'Okay, let him be.' "

Frisch's uneasiness, however, immediately proved warranted. The next batter hit a grounder to Gehringer, who flipped it to Rogell, who fired on to first base—only to find himself bouncing the peg right off the coconut of a 30-game winner.

"Dizzy had gone in standing up," Hallahan said. "Why, I don't know. I was going to ask him about it later, but by that time he'd already given ten different answers to ten different people. Anyway, he went down like he'd been shot. We all stood up in the dugout and you could just feel what everybody was thinking: there goes the Series."

Dizzy was carried off the field and whisked to the hospital. He showed up at the club's hotel that night hale and hearty, with a big grin on his face and a memorable line of reassurance: "They X-rayed my head and didn't find anything."

Pepper Martin grabbing some chaw. Note the centennial patch on Pepper's left sleeve.

A familiar face joins the 1934 World Series festivities. *Left to right:* Dizzy Dean, Frankie Frisch, Babe Ruth, and Detroit's Mickey Cochrane and Schoolboy Rowe.

Pepper lining one in the '34 Series. Cochrane is the catcher, Beans Reardon the umpire.

Pinch-runner Dizzy Dean using his head to break up a double play in the fourth inning of Game 4 of the 1934 World Series. Tiger shortstop Billy Rogell has just thrown the ball, fed by second baseman Charlie Gehringer (right).

Dizzy on the ground after being skulled by Rogell's throw. Frankie Frisch is kneeling over him.

The Tigers went up three games to two when Bridges beat Dizzy in Game 5, 3–1, sending the Series back to Detroit.

Paul Dean took the mound for St. Louis in Game 6 and, helped by three hits from the normally light-hitting Durocher, beat Rowe, 4–3, with Paul's own single knocking in Leo with the tie-breaker in the top of the seventh. That cleared the boards for a seventh game, and given the character of The Gashouse Gang, it is not surprising that the Series ended with a resounding rumpus.

Dizzy took the mound for the Cardinals, going on just one day's rest, against Auker. In the top of the third the Cardinals ripped it open with seven runs, casting a pall over the 40,000 Tiger fans who had been hoping for Detroit's first world championship.

In the top of the sixth, Medwick tripled in another run, and when Joe slid into third the

Tigers' Marv Owen thought it was with too much enthusiasm and he and Medwick squared off. The combatants were quickly separated, but when Joe went out to take his left-field position in the bottom of the inning he found himself the target of the frustrated bleacher fans, who seemed to have been waiting to erupt. They took dead aim at Joe with fruit, vegetables, soda pop bottles, and any other missile that would fly. As soon as stadium personnel cleaned up one mess, another came flying out.

"I don't know where they were getting all that stuff from," Charlie Gehringer said. "It was like they were backing produce trucks up to the gate and supplying everybody."

With the game unable to continue, Commissioner Landis summoned Medwick, Frisch, and the umpires to his box. There a decision was made to remove Joe from the game "to

Leo Durocher roaring home during the '34 Series. Tiger catcher Mickey Cochrane hasn't got a chance.

Joe Medwick's rambunctious, riot-provoking slide into Detroit third baseman Marv Owen in the sixth inning of Game 7 of the 1934 World Series.

(BELOW) A defiant Medwick standing in left field amid a shower of produce after his near-fight with Owen. Commissioner Landis was compelled to remove Joe from the field so order could be restored.

protect the player from injury and permit the game to continue." This action deprived the Cardinals of their top hitter, but with the score already 9–0 and Dizzy in top form, it made little difference. The final was 11–0 and a third World Championship for the Cardinals. Dizzy's prediction that "Me 'n Paul" would win two games apiece had been right on the money. It was a foregone conclusion that Dizzy would win the MVP Award, and he did, making him the second Cardinal in four years to be so honored.

The 1934 season marked high tide for The Gashouse Gang. Favored to win a year later, they played good ball, winning 96 games, but bumped into a September buzzsaw called the Chicago Cubs, who ran off a 21-game winning streak (the Cardinals themselves put together a club-record 14-game July win streak) during which they shot to the top and stayed there, finishing four games ahead of the second-place Cardinals.

(OPPOSITE TOP RIGHT) Joe Medwick posing in the dugout.

Jack Rothrock (1934–35), an outfielder who joined the Cardinals after eight years in the American League.

Wearing a different sort of uniform are Dizzy Dean *(left)* and Frankie Frisch doing the banquet circuit in the winter of 1934.

Left-hander Bill Walker (1933–36). He posted a 12–4 record in 1934.

Side-arming righty Tex Carleton (1932–34). His best was 17–11 in 1933.

Johnny Mize (1936–41). Big John averaged .336 in his six years as a Cardinal.

Outfielder Ernie Orsatti (1927–35). He hit for a lifetime average of .306 during his nine-year career with St. Louis.

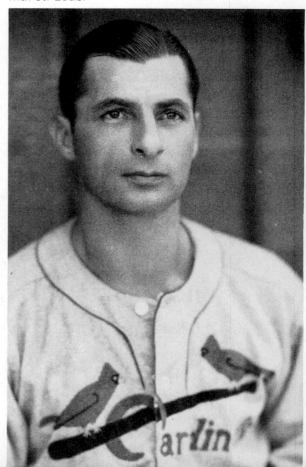

Hard-hitting catcher Virgil ("Spud") Davis (1928, 1934–36), who batted .317 for the Cards in 1935.

The Deans were again big winners—Dizzy 28–12, Paul 19–12—and Hallahan at 15–8 had his last productive year, but it wasn't enough. Chicago's ace was right-hander Bill Lee (20–6), who had been developed in the Cardinal system and then sold to the Cubs. Medwick batted .353, drove in 126 runs, and had 224 hits, running second in the league in each category. Collins batted .313 and knocked in 122 runs, but Rip's days as Cardinal first baseman were numbered, for that ever-fertile Redbird organization was about to turn out Big John Mize, greatest of all Cardinal first basemen.

The farm system sent up Terry Moore in 1935; he would soon have a reputation as a peerless defensive center fielder, with an arm so strong infielders said his pegs came in like cannon shots and "hurt." Terry batted .287 in his rookie year.

In 1936, the Cardinals again finished second (in a tie with the Cubs), but even so were a team that was closer to sunset than to sunrise. There were some gaudy achievements—Dizzy was 24–13; Medwick tore up opposing pitching with a .351 average, compiling league-leading figures in RBIs (138), hits (223), and doubles (64, still the league record); and rookie Mize broke in at first base with a .329 average.

But there were also a couple of serious misfortunes. After starting off well, Paul Dean injured his arm and was through at the age of twenty-three. In addition, the club's gifted young catcher, Bill DeLancey, had come down with tuberculosis the year before and not been able to make it back. At the age of twenty-four, he, too, was suddenly an ex–major leaguer. Frisch said, "You can't lose a catcher like that and not have it affect your entire ball club." In Rickey's estimation, DeLancey would have been one of the all-time great catchers. The luckless DeLancey died ten years later, on his thirty-fifth birthday.

Second baseman Burgess Whitehead (1933–35).

Paul (''Daffy'') Dean (1934–39). He might have thrown harder than his brother Dizzy, but he definitely talked softer.

Injuries and thirty-eight years of relentless wear and tear finally caught up to Frisch, and the skipper got into just 93 games, his final year of substantial playing time.

At the end of the season the club brought up minor league first baseman Walter Alston for a sip of coffee. The twenty-four-year-old Alston had one at bat, struck out, and then returned to the minor leagues, where he would play and manage until 1954, when he resurfaced to begin a 23-year career as manager of the Brooklyn and Los Angeles Dodgers.

Alston's brief stay with the Cardinals almost became footnoted in club history. While watching a card game in the clubhouse, he was told by one of the participants to "get the hell away." The speaker was Medwick.

"Joe didn't like rookies," Jesse Haines, who was there, said. "Joe could be nasty. He said something else to Walter, who just stood there staring at him. You could see that Walter was thinking it over. Then he thought better of it and walked away. And it was a damned good

Catcher Bill Delancey (1932, 1934–35, 1940), *(left)*, and Paul Dean.

Walter Alston (1936). One at bat with the Cardinals, one strikeout. That was the sum total of Alston's big-league career as a player. He later managed the Dodgers in Brooklyn and Los Angeles for 23 years.

of string to a dollar bill and sit in a hotel lobby and snatch the buck away from the fingers of those who bent for it, and cigars continued to explode in the Cardinal clubhouse. On a broiling, 100-degree St. Louis afternoon several Gashousers emerged in fur coats and built a fire in front of the dugout.

Music would come from Pepper's "Mudcat Band," which featured Martin on harmonica and guitar, Lon Warneke on guitar, left-hander Bob Weiland blowing into a cloudy jug, outfielder Frenchy Bordagaray on a setup that included a washboard, whistle, and automobile horn, and pitcher Bill McGee on a broken-down fiddle (it earned him the nickname "Fiddler Bill"). They played semblances of cowboy and hillbilly tunes and they sang and cavorted and wore outlandish outfits (including a grass skirt for Pepper), while Frisch lamented that he was "the only manager who travels with his own orchestra."

thing he did. Joe was tough, but Walter would have torn him to pieces. Walter was strong, as strong as any man I ever met in my life. But he always had good sense, and I guess he figured it wouldn't look good for a rookie to come in and take apart the team's star hitter."

The Gashouse Gang was still in full spirit. Their classic caper involved Dizzy, Pepper, and Ripper Collins. One rainy afternoon, with their game postponed, the trio donned overalls and box-shaped carpenters' caps and, carrying ladders and hammers, invaded the banquet hall at their hotel, the swank Bellevue-Stratford in Philadelphia, where a large, stately dinner was in progress. Dean set up a ladder, climbed it, and began hammering on the ceiling, while his cohorts were rearranging furniture and crawling under tables. The toastmasters and diners were outraged—until the intruders were recognized, whereupon they were applauded and invited to join the occasion and were seated at the head table.

Pepper continued to drop bags of water from hotel windows, Dizzy would tape a long piece

Jesse Haines, in 1934, still pitching for the Cardinals after fifteen years.

Bob Weiland (1937–40). He won 16 games in 1938.

In 1937, the two most famous Cardinals took opposite journeys, one to baseball's pinnacle, the other to the basement with a career-ending injury. For Joe Medwick it was a blistering summer of Triple Crown hitting: .374 batting average, 31 home runs, 154 runs batted in, in addition to league-high marks in runs (111), doubles (56), hits (237), total bases (406), and slugging (.641). In becoming the third St. Louis Cardinal to carry off the MVP Award, Joe had turned in the kind of explosive hitting Hornsby had racked up in the 1920s and another Cardinal, Stan Musial, would deliver in the 1940s. Medwick was paced all season long by sophomore Johnny Mize, who batted .364 and finished second to Joe in batting, slugging, total bases, and doubles. But this lethal duo notwithstanding, the best the team could manage was fourth place.

The injury occurred to Dizzy Dean. Selected to start for the National League in the All-Star Game at Washington's Griffith Stadium, Dean had almost completed his three-inning stint when Cleveland's Earl Averill rifled a low blur

Outfielder Stanley ("Frenchy") Bordagaray (1937–38), one of the game's blithe spirits. He batted .293 in 1937.

Right-hander Bill McGee (1935–41). He won 16 games in 1940.

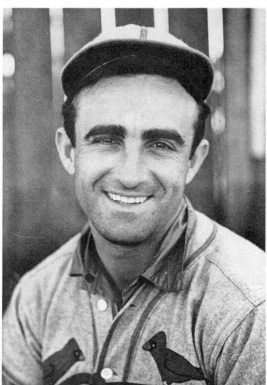

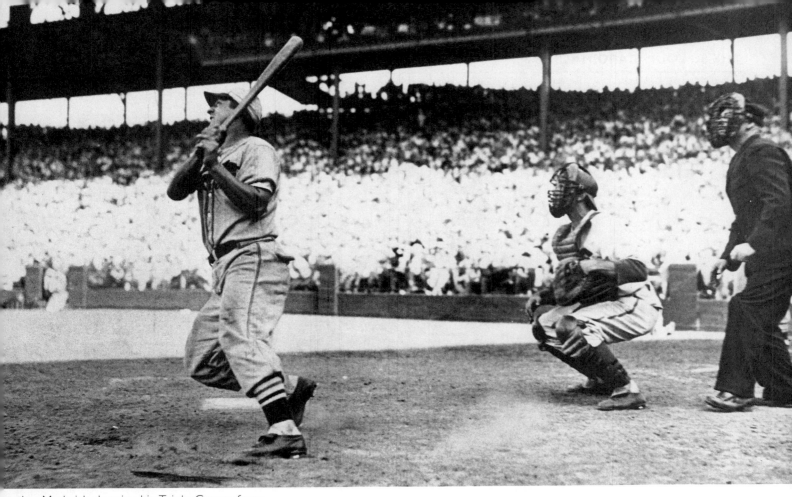

Joe Medwick showing his Triple Crown form.

Engaged in a different sort of game are, *(left to right)*, Dizzy Dean, Lon Warneke, and Leo Durocher.

Dizzy Dean making it an unforgettable moment for a group of young fans.

Rookie Enos ("Country") Slaughter *(center)* joins Johnny Mize *(left)* and Pepper Martin at the batting cage in spring training, 1938.

of a line drive right back at the mound. The missile rammed into Dizzy's right foot and broke a toe.

Less than two weeks later Dizzy was back on the mound, pitching against Bill Mc-Kechnie's Boston Braves. Conflicting stories surround Dean's obviously premature return to the mound. One story has it that the club did not want its biggest drawing card idled for very long, another that Dean insisted on pitching. Whatever the facts, common sense should have prevailed and the club's most valuable commodity should not have been allowed to return to work before he was fully healed.

Favoring the still painful toe, Dean was throwing with an unnatural motion. McKechnie spotted this and urged him not to pitch. But Dizzy

Dean was twenty-six years old, headstrong, grandly self-confident, possessor of the most magnetic right arm in America. He assured McKechnie it was all right. A few innings into the game, something in that right arm snapped: Some say it was the elastic in the slingshot that propelled the missiles. Whatever it was, that thrilling fastball never whistled again.

Dean did not win another game that season, ending with a 13–10 record. The following spring Rickey sold him to the Cubs for $185,000, the Cubs fully understanding they were receiving the shadow and not the monument, but the idea of owning Dizzy Dean, even a Dizzy Dean whose fastball was as lethal as a cabbage, was too much of a temptation to let pass. Using guile and slow curves, Dizzy was

7-1 for the Cubs in 1938, helping them to a pennant. Soon after, though, he was through.

The Cardinals' 1938 season was one of those transitional years for a ball club, more recognizable in retrospect than at the time. Personnel was changing and so was personality; a "Gashouse Gang" didn't quite fit on a sixth-place team, which the Cardinals were in 1938, and anyway erosion was gnawing at those marauders and their talents. Dizzy and Ripper were gone (the latter traded to the Cubs for right-hander Lon Warneke), Pepper was no longer a regular, Durocher had been traded to Brooklyn, and in September the skipper himself, Frankie Frisch, was fired. Breadon told Frisch, "I hate to do this," and even though clubowners always say this to their departing managers, Sam probably meant it. Frisch had proven a pivotal man in Cardinal history and Breadon was grateful, especially for the way Frankie had come in and replaced the "irre-

Infielder Don Gutteridge (1936–40), (left), and manager Frankie Frisch.

Playing second base most of the time, Stu Martin was with the Cardinals from 1936 through 1940. A .298 batting average in 1936 was his best.

placeable" Hornsby in 1927. (Frisch took over as manager of the Pirates in 1940.)

Joe Medwick slipped from his Triple Crown season, which in Joe's case meant a .322 batting average, 21 home runs, and a league-leading 122 RBIs, good enough for a third straight title, a major league record he shares with several others. Mize batted .337 and led with 16 triples and a .614 slugging average.

But even as the Gashousers were folding their tents, the Cardinal farm system continued to deliver its harvest. Playing right field this year was rookie Enos Slaughter, a man who would soon become his era's symbol of fervent, nonstop hustle. If there was a prototypical Cardinal, it was Slaughter. He was tough, daring, absolutely dedicated to making that 360-foot trip around the bases as quickly as possible. He could run, he possessed a strong arm; he was a Carolina country boy and he was a hungry player, willing to take chances.

Si Johnson (1936–38). He had a 12–12 record in 1937.

No player ever brought more devotion to the game nor to his employers—when at last it came time for Slaughter and the Cardinals to part company in 1954, Enos broke down and wept.

The rays of the future were also shining through the cracks in the wall in the person of a couple of young pitchers soon to make their presence felt—right-hander Mort Cooper, who broke into a few games and soon would be the ace, and lefty Max Lanier, a youngster with a live fastball. Another young southpaw, Preacher Roe, also surfaced from the system, but the Cardinals were soon to be so player-rich that Roe would be forced to find stardom elsewhere.

The farm system received a body blow that year from Commissioner Landis. The judge had never liked Rickey (those luxuriant egos could never mesh), nor did he approve of a farm system, seeing it as a threat to the independently owned minor league teams. But since Rickey's concept did not in any way contravene baseball law, there was nothing that the old authoritarian Landis could do about it—until 1938, when he found the Cardinals were committing various infractions of baseball regulations such as contract manipulation, "secret" arrangements with certain minor league teams, and impeding the progress of certain young players (by some estimates, the Cardinals had close to 800 players under contract). Accordingly, Landis "liberated" 74 members of the St. Louis "chain gang," declaring them free agents. Among them was the abundantly gifted outfielder Pete Reiser, Rickey's "jewel of the organization," and "the most naturally gifted young player I have ever seen." Reiser signed with Brooklyn—for a $100 bonus—and by 1941 was the National League batting champion.

The new manager was Ray Blades, who had spent his big league career (1922–32) in the St. Louis Cardinal outfield, most of it in a backup

(OPPOSITE RIGHT) Enos Slaughter (1938–42, 1946–53), the Cardinals' longtime symbol of hustle and desire.

Curt Davis (1938–40), who was a 22-game winner for St. Louis in 1939.

Ray Blades, the Cardinals' outfielder from the 1920s, who returned as manager in 1939–40.

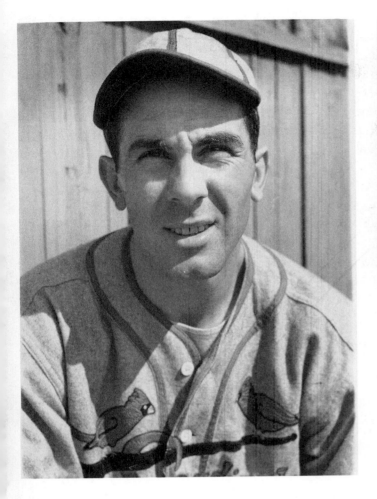

(ABOVE) Catcher Mickey Owen (1937–40), who was sold to the Brooklyn Dodgers to make way for Walker Cooper.

(LEFT) Southpaw Clyde Shoun (1938–42), one of the Cardinals' top relievers. He led the league in appearances in 1939 and 1940. A rugged character, he was known as "Hardrock."

(BELOW) *Left to right:* Don Padgett, Johnny Mize, Enos Slaughter, and Terry Moore.

role. Blades had served his managerial apprenticeship at Columbus, Ohio, and Rochester. The feisty Blades made his club the surprise of the year in 1939 as the Cardinals chased the Cincinnati Reds all summer and, winning 92 games, finished second, 4½ games behind. The difference lay in Cincinnati's two big pitchers, Bucky Walters, who won 27, and ex-Cardinal Paul Derringer, a 25-game winner.

For the Cardinals, sidewheeling right-hander Curt Davis was 22–16, but after Davis the top winners were Bob Bowman and Lon Warneke with 13 apiece and Mort Cooper with 12.

The team's .294 batting average easily led the league, as did their 779 runs and 332 doubles. Mize won two corners of the Triple Crown with 28 home runs and a .349 batting average, Medwick batted .332, and Slaughter was at .320 and had 52 doubles, tops in the league. Backup catcher Don Padgett (Mickey Owen was the regular) broke into 92 games and used his 233 at bats to register a soaring .399 average.

So for the Cardinals the decade closed on a high note of promise. In the 1930s the team had won three pennants and two World Championships. A new cast of young and hungry Redbirds would do even better in the coming decade.

F·I·V·E

ENTER STAN THE MAN

THE FARM SYSTEM WAS NOW poised for peak production, with the Cardinals about to start reaping a harvest of wealth and abundance. Marty Marion, good enough to become known as "Mr. Shortstop," took over that position in 1940, beginning a dominant ten-year career. Outfielder Harry Walker and catcher Walker Cooper (brother of Mort) broke in briefly, as did pitchers Harry Brecheen, Ernie White, and Murry Dickson, all of whom were going to help shape the club's coming years.

The 1940 season, however, proved a disappointment for Cardinal fans. Expected to contend, the team finished third, 16 games behind the Reds. Veteran right-handers Bill McGee and Lon Warneke each won 16 games, but the staff lacked a true ace. Mize hit 43 home runs, leading the league and setting a team record that still stands; the big man also led in RBIs with 137. Slaughter and Moore batted over .300, as did part-timer Pepper Martin, who left after the season to manage at Sacramento, moving the Cardinals still further away from the Gashouse days.

On June 12, the Cardinals engineered a deal with Brooklyn that stunned many of their fans. As they had done with Hornsby in 1926, the club suddenly unloaded their top hitter, Joe Medwick, and this time received no Frankie Frisch in return. In exchange for Medwick and Curt Davis, the Cardinals received four also-rans and a check for $125,000.

The Cardinals had their reasons for disposing of their twenty-eight-year-old slugger. Joe and the team were both off to disappointing starts, he had been sniping at Blades for send-

Shortstop Marty Marion (1940–50). They called him "Slats" and "The Octopus." They also called him the top shortstop of his era.

ing in late-inning defensive replacements for him, he was disgruntled over the $2,000 Breadon had trimmed from his contract in 1939 (after Joe had batted .322 and led the league in RBIs), and, ever outspoken, had been letting the boss in on his feelings. When the Cardinals

(TOP LEFT) Johnny Mize, who hit 43 homers in 1940, is the last Cardinal to lead the league in home runs.

(TOP RIGHT) Joe Medwick in 1940, shortly before he was dealt to the Dodgers. (The background is Brooklyn's Ebbets Field.)

(LEFT) Manager Ray Blades (left) and his star hitter, Joe Medwick.

drew only 23,000 for their much-trumpeted first night game at Sportsman's Park on June 4, Sam's mood became testy and a week later Medwick was gone, dealt to Brooklyn, where Larry MacPhail had taken over as general manager (hiring Durocher as manager) and was wheeling, dealing, and spending to build a winner as quickly as possible.

Shortly after the transaction, the Cardinals were at Ebbets Field and Medwick was batting against his former teammates when right-hander Bob Bowman bounced a high hard one off of Joe's head. These were pre-batting helmet days and Joe keeled over like a lead weight and was carried off the field. The volatile MacPhail accused Bowman of having deliberately beaned Joe (Medwick and Bowman reportedly had exchanged hostile words in a hotel earlier in the day) and wanted the pitcher indicted for attempted manslaughter. Bowman was spirited out of town, to protect him not from the DA but from the wrath of irate Brooklyn fans, never a placid lot under the best of circumstances. Bowman was not indicted and Medwick never again was the line-drive machine he had been before the beaning.

Breadon became impatient with the team and, over Rickey's protests, canned Ray Blades early in June. Blades' replacement was former manager Billy Southworth, then running the Rochester club.

The forty-seven-year-old Southworth was a popular choice. He had known many of the players in the minor leagues and was highly regarded. Billy was a low-key man, considerate of his players; he was patient and understanding, and at the same time an extremely shrewd and sound baseball man.

When Southworth took over, the club was laboring under a 15–29 record; after that, Billy led them to a 69–40 record and Cardinal fans began looking forward to next year.

The 1941 season proved to be a critical turning point for the Cardinals. Despite a series of crippling injuries, Southworth's men fought a grueling season-long pennant race with Durocher's Dodgers that didn't end until the Dodgers clinched it in their 152nd game, end-

Right-hander Bob Bowman (1939–40), the man who beaned Medwick. He was 13–5 in 1939, but soon faded.

ing with a 2½-game margin over the Cardinals, who won 97 games, at that time second highest in their history. The race also attracted over 633,000 fans, almost double 1940's attendance.

Brooklyn's champions had a definite St. Louis tinge to their lineup: in addition to Medwick were Pete Reiser, the former Cardinal farmhand "freed" by Landis, flourishing with a .343 league-leading average; catcher Mickey Owen, purchased from the Cardinals for $60,000; Curt Davis, 13–7 for the Dodgers; and the skipper himself, Leo Durocher.

Southworth kept his men in the race until the end despite the following: a broken finger suffered by Mize, which caused the big man's home run output to drop from 43 to 16; mid-season elbow surgery that deprived the club of their best pitcher, Mort Cooper, for six weeks; a broken collarbone by Walker Cooper that limited the big catcher to 68 games; another broken collarbone, this one suffered by Slaughter in an outfield collision with Moore on August 10; and then two weeks later Moore was severely beaned, further depleting the lineup.

Mort Cooper (1938–45). He was the Cardinal ace in the early 1940s.

Another twenty-year-old who broke in under conditions of year-end pennant pressure was outfielder Stanley Musial.

"Pressure?" Ernie White said when speaking of Musial. "I don't think anyone ever explained to him what it meant. We were fighting for our lives and this kid comes up cool as ice and starts hitting line drives that made the ball bleed."

In 12 games, the youngster who would soon become the league's greatest hitter since Hornsby came to bat 47 times and rapped 20 hits for a .426 batting average. Years later, Johnny Mize echoed the feelings of many of the Cardinals when he said, "If they would have brought Musial up earlier we would have won the pennant in 1941."

Musial was one of those rare players who is

Typical of the Dodger-Cardinal games that year was the one played before a packed house at Sportsman's Park on September 13. With the Dodgers holding a one-game lead, Brooklyn ace Whitlow Wyatt outdueled Cooper, 1–0. Cooper had a no-hitter until the top of the eighth, when Dixie Walker and Billy Herman cracked back-to-back doubles for the game's only run.

The near-miss in 1941 was disappointing, but nevertheless left the Cardinals feeling confident about 1942. Left-hander Ernie White had blossomed with a 17–7 record, while Warneke was 17–9, with the veteran pitching a 2–0 no-hitter against the Reds on August 30. Reliever Howie Krist was 10–0, and up from Houston late in the season came left-hander Howie Pollett. Debuting in the cauldron of a pennant race, the twenty-year-old Pollett was 5–2 with a 1.93 ERA.

Left-hander Ernie White (1940–43). A sore arm curtailed this fine pitcher's career.

Howie Krist (1937–38, 1941–43, 1946), who was a perfect 10–0 as a starter and reliever in 1941.

Armed with all the tools, young Stan Musial is set to play in 1942.

Right-hander Lon Warneke (1937–42). Three times a 20-game winner for the Cubs in the 1930s, Lon won 18 for the Cardinals in 1937 and 17 in 1941.

so good that even his birthplace—Donora, Pennsylvania—becomes well-known. He entered the Cardinal organization in 1938, a seventeen-year-old left-handed pitcher. He did moderately well for a couple of years, then in 1940 was 18–5 for Daytona Beach in the Florida State League when he injured his left shoulder making a tumbling catch in the outfield (where, because of his live bat, the club was playing him between starts).

Once Musial gave up pitching and became a full-time outfielder, his rise through the organization was swift. He began the 1941 season with Springfield in the West Virginia League, batted .379 in 87 games, and was elevated to the top farm club at Rochester. In this big league anteroom the slender youngster with the snapping, flawless left-handed swing batted .326 in 54 games, and then was summoned to St. Louis for the season's final weeks.

No superstar in baseball history was ever more genuine, more unaffected, more engaging, more widely and sincerely liked.

"You could make a study of Musial's life," Rickey once said, "and learn how to be a decent human being. He did not have a shred of ego or temperament. He was always serene, no matter the situation. How he was able to maintain this serenity, this calm, and be at all times the most self-confident, highly concentrated, and zealous competitor that he also was, is surely worth reflecting upon."

In time Musial would break many of Honus Wagner's National League hitting records, posting fresh numbers for later-day hitters such as Hank Aaron and Pete Rose to peck away at.

The city of St. Louis embraced "Stan the Man" with a municipal bear hug. (The famous nickname came from Dodger fans watching Musial rattle line drives around their beloved Ebbets Field. It got to the point where they would moan and say, "Here comes the Man again." The nickname caught on instantly.) Musial was the Cardinals' fourth true superstar. Hornsby had offended people with his blunt candor, Medwick with his surliness, and even the lovable Dean had found detractors with his bragging and his bursts of temperament.

The ever-friendly Musial, however, was "perfect." And, as one writer added, "That goes for off the field as well as on."

The 1942 St. Louis Cardinals are remembered by those who saw them play as one of baseball's greatest all-time teams. The claim is not borne out by statistics, for the '42 Cardinals batted a modest .268 (best in the league) and hit just 60 home runs. Slaughter led the team with a .318 average, 13 home runs, and 98 RBIs. Musial batted .315. No other regular hit over .300.

The pitching was superb. Mort Cooper was 22–7 with ten shutouts and a league-leading 1.77 ERA. Farm system graduate Johnny Beazley was 21–6 in his rookie year. Howie Krist was 13–3, Max Lanier 13–8. The staff ERA was 2.55, lowest in baseball since 1919 (the last year of the dead ball) and not to be bettered until 1967.

Johnny Beazley (1941–42, 1946). Injuries aborted what might have been one of the outstanding pitching careers in Cardinal history.

Max Lanier (1938–46, 1949–51), the talented lefty who interrupted his big-league career when he jumped to the Mexican League in 1946. His best year in the bigs was 1944, when he was 17–12.

Utility outfielder Coaker Triplett (1941–43).

Gus Mancuso (*left*), back for a second hitch with the Cardinals in 1941, and outfielder Ernie Koy (1940–41), a speedster who came to St. Louis from Brooklyn in the Medwick deal.

What was remarkable about this team was their unity, the single-minded purpose with which they took the field. Few clubs have ever attacked with such élan or such pure baseball sense. This esprit de corps derived in large part from the fact that virtually every man on the club had risen from the farm system, had been trained to play, think, and react in a certain way. It was a young, hungry, daring team that refused to believe it could be beaten, and that, finally, in the end, was not beaten, because they ran out every grounder, dove for every ball, and took every extra base.

Adding luster to the '42 Cardinals was the way they won their pennant and the quality of the team they beat. The 1942 Dodgers were a first-rate team, as tough and determined as the Cardinals. But in 1942 it was St. Louis that possessed the ultimate kick and stamina that characterizes the successful long-distance runner. When it was over, Brooklyn had won 104

games—a princely total—but Southworth's relentless crew had won 106.

With Mize having been sold to the New York Giants the previous December, the Cardinals went with a first-base tandem of Ray Sanders and Johnny Hopp. Second base was manned by Frank ("Creepy") Crespi and Jimmy Brown. Shortstop belonged to Marion and third base to the rugged Whitey Kurowski. The outfield was Musial, Moore, and Slaughter, while Walker Cooper was behind the plate, forming one of baseball's great brother batteries with his brother Mort, who would be voted MVP.

The Dodgers led the league for much of the season, and in early August were up by ten games. At this point, MacPhail came into the clubhouse and accused his players of complacency, warning them that the Cardinals had not given up. He was told not to worry.

By the end of August the Cardinals had

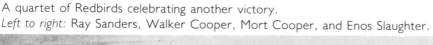

A quartet of Redbirds celebrating another victory.
Left to right: Ray Sanders, Walker Cooper, Mort Cooper, and Enos Slaughter.

trimmed the lead to 7½, with the Dodgers coming into St. Louis for a four-game series. Lanier, 5–2 against the Dodgers that year, won the opener. The next day Cooper and Whitlow Wyatt staged another one of their tense duels, with Cooper winning in 14 innings, 2–1. Beazley won the next day, but the Dodgers won the last game and left town with a 5½-game lead.

By the time the Cardinals came into Ebbets Field for a two-game set on September 11 and 12, the Dodger lead had withered to two games. Cooper fired a 3–0 shutout to win the first game and Lanier followed with a 2–1 beauty the next day, both runs coming on a Kurowski homer. The teams were now in a first-place tie.

The next day the Dodgers lost a double-header to the Reds while the Cardinals went into first place by sweeping the Phillies. From there on it was one rabbit chasing another. Both clubs played brilliantly down the stretch, but the Cardinals were never caught. At one

The feisty Jimmy Brown, who played all over the in-field for the Cards from 1937 through 1943.

The heart of manager Billy Southworth's pitching staff in 1942. *Left to right:* Max Lanier, Ernie White, Mort Cooper, Johnny Beazley, and Harry Gumbert.

A jubilant cast of Cardinals after winning the second game of the 1942 World Series. *Front, left:* Billy Southworth and Walker Cooper. *Rear, left to right:* Enos Slaughter, Stan Musial, winning pitcher Johnny Beazley, and Whitey Kurowski.

point, the Dodgers won eight straight and still lost ground.

St. Louis, with a final margin of two games—each of their five pennants had been won by the same margin—had put on a blistering drive that actually consisted of one third of the season as they won 43 of their last 51 games. Their September record was 21–4, Brooklyn's 20–5.

The Cardinals kept their momentum going into and right on through the World Series. Their opponents were Joe McCarthy's New York Yankees, an all-consuming lion's jaw of a team that had taken its sixth pennant in seven years. These were the Yankees of Joe Di-

Maggio, Bill Dickey, Charlie Keller, Phil Rizzuto, Joe Gordon, and strong pitchers like Red Ruffing, Ernie Bonham, Hank Borowy, and Spud Chandler. The New Yorkers were heavily favored to win.

Ruffing beat Cooper and the Cardinals in the opener in St. Louis, 7–4, pitching no-hit ball into the eighth inning. The four St. Louis runs came in a spirited ninth inning rally that left the Cardinals brimming with optimism.

"We'd thrown a scare into the Yankees," Ernie White said, "and even though we'd lost, we couldn't wait to get back out on the field the next day."

Beazley won Game 2, 4–3, and the Series

The starting pitchers for Game 3 of the 1942 World Series: St. Louis's Ernie White (*left*) and New York's Spud Chandler.

Enjoying a Cardinal triumph are, (*left to right*), Frank Crespi, outfielder Estel Crabtree (1933, 1941–42), and Ernie White.

moved to Yankee Stadium, traditionally a graveyard for visiting ball clubs with high aspirations. But nothing could intimidate this Cardinal outfit, most of whom felt they had already played their most daunting games of the season—against Brooklyn at Ebbets Field in September.

Ernie White pitched the game of his life in Game 3. Suffering with a sore arm all season, White delivered a 3–0 shutout, with Musial in left field taking a home run away from Gordon with a leaping catch and Slaughter robbing Keller with an even more spectacular leap in right, on successive pitches in the seventh inning.

In Game 4, the Cardinals went toe-to-toe with the Yankees and outslugged the sluggers, 9–6, with Lanier hurling three innings of airtight relief to seal it. The Cardinals completed their dazzling upset the next day behind Beazley, 4–2. The winning runs came on Whitey Kurowski's two-run homer in the top of the ninth, a blow that ranks in Cardinal history with Whitey's September blast against Brooklyn.

Third baseman Whitey Kurowski (1941–49). In '42 he hit two of the biggest home runs in Cardinal history.

Only eight years removed from The Gashouse Gang world champions of 1934, this was an altogether different cast of Cardinal champions. They were every bit as tough and daring as Frisch's roistering scrappers; the difference was there were no hijinks, no Mudcat Band, no practical jokes. Maybe it was because they had grown up and learned their trade during the hard years of the Depression, competing with hundreds of other boys for those few, precious jobs at the top. And there was the grimness of war, too, now, which America had been bombed into at Pearl Harbor the previous December. After the exciting summer and triumphant autumn of 1942, the St. Louis Cardinals, like the rest of baseball and the rest of the country, headed into years of peril and uncertainty.

Appreciating its recreational value for a nation at war, President Franklin Delano Roosevelt encouraged the game to continue, and baseball did, though like an old tire it kept acquiring more and more patches to keep it going.

The first significant departure from the Cardinals occurred a month after the 1942 World Series, and though it was war-related, it probably would have taken place anyway. The man whose name had become synonymous with Cardinal success, Branch Rickey, was leaving St. Louis and going to Brooklyn, where he would be succeeding Larry MacPhail as club president, MacPhail having talked himself into a lieutenant colonelcy and gone off to war.

The severing of the nearly quarter-century relationship between Breadon and Rickey was amicable, though Sam was probably not sorry to see Branch go. For one thing, Rickey was drawing a large salary, and with the uncertainties of war lying ahead, Breadon wasn't sure if he would be able to afford his high-priced chief executive. For another thing, the newspapers were constantly praising Rickey's acumen in building a championship club (and Branch was never shy about accepting kudos), and even though Breadon had always recognized and appreciated Rickey's abilities, the owner felt that his own contributions were being overlooked. And so Rickey departed for Brooklyn, where he would build another immensely productive farm system and help the Dodgers win six pennants in a ten-year span (1947–56).

By 1943, big league rosters began to feel the impact of the war. Among the first Cardinals to join the armed services were Crespi, Moore, Slaughter, and Beazley. (Beazley was to hurt his arm pitching for a service team during the war and the talented right-hander never regained the brilliance he had shown in his rookie year.) In July, Jimmy Brown departed, as did Pollett, whose last three starts were shutout victories.

Born in St. Louis, Frank ("Creepy") Crespi played second base for his hometown club from 1938 through 1942, with 1941 his only full season.

Moore and Slaughter were replaced by Danny Litwhiler, acquired in a trade with the Phillies, and Harry Walker. Farm product Lou Klein took over at second, and the organization also coughed up three quality pitchers in George Munger and left-handers Harry Brecheen and Alpha Brazle.

What began as a close race in the National League came apart in July, with the Cardinals pulling steadily away and ending with their greatest victory margin ever, an 18-game bulge over second-place Cincinnati, built on a 105–49 record. Musial enjoyed his first great year, leading the league in batting (.357), hits (220), doubles (48), triples (20), slugging (.562), and total bases (347). He was easily the league's MVP, with Walker Cooper (.319) the runner-up. The infield was a model of consistency:

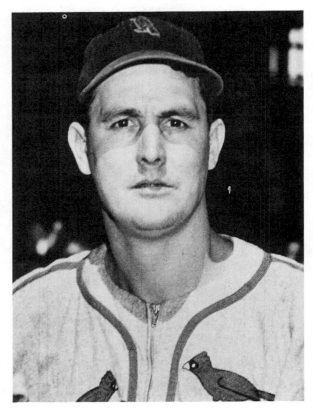

Mort Cooper.

One of the Cardinals' top catchers of all time, Walker Cooper (1940–45, 1956–57).

Sanders batted .280, Klein .287, Marion .280, and Kurowski .287.

Mort Cooper again topped Southworth's staff, posting a 21–8 record, including a pair of back-to-back one-hitters against the Dodgers on May 31 and Phillies on June 4. Lanier was next on the staff with a 15–7 record. Pollett, who was 8–4 before leaving, had the league's lowest ERA, 1.75, followed by Lanier's 1.90 and Cooper's 2.30. The staff's combined 2.57 ERA was easily the league's best.

The 1943 World Series was a rematch, McCarthy's Yankees having won again in the American League. Like the Cardinals, the Yankees had lost some of their stars to the military, including DiMaggio, Rizzuto, and Ruffing.

For the second straight year, it was a five-game Series, but this time the New Yorkers won it. Yankee ace Spud Chandler defeated Lanier in the opener, 4–2. Cooper won a 4–3 game the following day, and then the Yankees went on to win 6–2, 2–1, and 2–0, Chandler pitching the shutout in the finale.

(ABOVE) *Left to right:* Harry Walker, Whitey Kurowski, Lou Klein, and Stan Musial.

(OPPOSITE TOP) A controversial call in the sixth inning of the opening game of the 1943 World Series. At Yankee Stadium, New York's Frank Crosetti has not yet touched the bag, while first baseman Ray Sanders has the ball—or seems to. Umpire Beans Reardon called Crosetti safe, igniting a heated argument. The play was important, as it led to a two-run inning for the Yankees, who went on to win the game 4–2.

(OPPOSITE BOTTOM) It's the eighth inning of Game 3 of the '43 World Series. Yankee baserunner Johnny Lindell (No. 18) has just bowled over Kurowski (on ground) at third base. Cardinal pitcher Al Brazle is walking over to check on his fallen teammate. The umpire is Bill Stewart. No. 31 is Yankee coach Art Schulte. Lindell would later join the Cardinals in 1950.

Major league players continued departing for military service, and Cardinal losses before the 1944 season included Walker, Klein, and pitchers Al Brazle, Howie Krist, and Ernie White, while George Munger left in midseason with an 11–3 record. Replacements included right-hander Ted Wilks, discharged from the Army because of an ulcer, who was 17–4, and second baseman Emil Verban.

Southworth's club tore through the league with a 105–49 record—same as the year before—and easily took their third straight pennant, finishing 14½ ahead of second-place Pittsburgh. The Cardinals remain the only National League team to have 100 victories in three straight seasons. On June 10, they emerged explosively from a slump that had seen them score just one run in 25 innings by burying the Reds in the most one-sided shutout

Terry Moore (*left*) and skipper Billy Southworth surveying the scene at spring training.

Stan Musial, the most popular of all the Cardinals.

victory in club history, 18–0. The onslaught was responsible for the making of a bit of baseball history. With the game far out of reach, Reds manager Bill McKechnie brought to the mound the youngest player in major league history—left-hander Joe Nuxhall, who was two months short of his 16th birthday. The youngster pitched two thirds of an inning, yielding two hits, five walks, and five runs. (That was it for the year for Joe, but he returned to the bigs in 1952 to begin a long, successful career.)

The Cardinals, who set a club record with 26 wins in July, led by as many as 20 games at the end of August. They were topped by Musial, who batted .347 (finishing second to Brooklyn's Dixie Walker) and led in slugging (.549), hits (197), and doubles (51). Johnny Hopp batted .336 and Walker Cooper .317, while the MVP Award went for the third straight year to a Cardinal, Marty Marion winning it this time (by one vote over Chicago's Bill Nicholson).

Mort Cooper delivered another big season, with a 22–7 record, followed by 17-game winners Wilks and Lanier, and a 16–5 year from Brecheen. The staff's 2.67 ERA led the league

Ted Wilks (1944–51), who broke in with a 17–4 record and later became an outstanding relief pitcher for the Cardinals.

Marty Marion, who was the National League's MVP in 1944.

The Cardinals and Browns not only shared the same city but also the same ballpark, and so the entire Series was played at Sportsman's Park. It was dubbed "The Trolley Car World Series" for the then-popular mode of transportation that carried fans to and from the ball park. The two clubs also, it seemed, shared many of the same fans. There was little of the intracity rivalry and hostility that had built up through the years between the fans of other multiteam cities such as New York and Chicago.

"The Browns had been such harmless bumblers for so many years," one writer said, "that

This is how bad it got during the war: Even the Cardinals, once the most player-rich organization in baseball, were reduced to advertising for players. This ad appeared in *The Sporting News* in February 1945.

for the third straight year. The team also led in runs, doubles, home runs, batting, slugging, and set a new major league record for fewest errors, 112. Helping to fill out the wartime roster was a familiar face—Pepper Martin. The now forty-year-old former Gashouser returned after a three-year absence and got into 40 games and batted .279.

For the first and only time in baseball history, the World Series was an all–St. Louis affair, the Browns having won on the last day of the season the only pennant they would ever win in their 52-year American League tenure (they became the Baltimore Orioles in 1954).

Righty Harry Gumbert (1941–44). Acquired from the Giants, he was the only player on the 1942 pennant-winning Cardinals who hadn't come up through the farm system.

hitter in the opener, Cooper lost to Denny Galehouse, 2–1. The Cardinals won an 11-inning thriller the next day, 3–2, behind the tight pitching of Lanier and reliever Blix Donnelly. In Game 3, the Browns roughed up Wilks with a four-run third inning and went on to win, 6–2.

First baseman–outfielder Johnny Hopp (1939–45). He batted .336 in 1944.

they had never bothered anybody and the city was kind of charmed by the fact that they had finally won a pennant."

Browns manager Luke Sewell noted the air of mixed emotion that hovered over the Series.

"It was the quietest World Series ever," Sewell said. "I don't think the fans knew who to root for. They'd been waiting all their lives for this and when it finally came to be, they just sat and took it all in without too much cheering."

The Cardinals were favored to win, and they did, but not before the Browns had taken two of the first three games. Despite pitching a two-

Ray Sanders, Cardinal first baseman from 1942 to 1945. He drove in 102 runs in 1944.

From then on, Cardinal pitching closed down the pesky Brownie bats, allowing just two runs over the final three games. Brecheen took Game 4, 5–1, sent winging by Musial's two-run homer in the first inning. In Game 5, Mort Cooper hurled a 2–0 shutout, the Cardinals scoring on solo homers by Sanders and Litwhiler. The finale saw Lanier and Wilks hold the Browns to just three hits in a 3–1 victory that gave the Cardinals their fifth World Championship and second in three years.

In a Series not noted for its hitting, Emil Verban was a standout. The Cardinal second baseman, a .257 hitter during the season, rapped out seven hits (all singles) in 17 at bats for a .412 average.

Southworth and the Cardinals were out to make history in 1945—a fourth straight pennant would have tied the record then held by John McGraw and his 1921–24 Giants (in whose outfield Billy had played in 1924) and Joe McCarthy's 1936–39 Yankees. The Cards fell short, however, as the Chicago Cubs, helped by a staff of veteran pitchers (which included St. Louis's one-time rookie star Paul Derringer), kept a few lengths ahead of the Cardinals all season and finally won the pennant by three games, despite the fact that St.

Emil Verban (1944–46), who filled in at second base for the Cardinals during the war.

One of the most popular of all Cardinals, Red Schoendienst (1945–56, 1961–63; manager 1965–76).

Red Barrett (1945–46), who was 23-12 in 1945. He was strictly a wartime ace.

Right-hander Ken Burkhart (1945–48), who was 19–8 in his rookie year.

Reserve catcher Ken O'Dea (1942–46).

Louis defeated Chicago 16 times in 22 meetings.

St. Louis losses to the military in this last wartime year included Musial, Walker Cooper, Litwhiler, and, early in the season, Lanier. In addition, Breadon had a contract dispute with Mort Cooper, the consequence of which was the ace being dealt to the Braves for $60,000 and right-hander Charley (Red) Barrett. Hitherto a mediocre performer, Barrett gave the Cardinals one big year—23–12—and nearly pitched them to a pennant. Rookie right-hander Ken Burkhart also gave the club his best year—19–8.

Another addition to the club this year proved to be significant and enduring. Up from Rochester came a switch-hitting, twenty-two-year old shortstop named Albert ("Red") Schoendienst. An easy-going youngster with a friendly Huckleberry Finn face, Schoendienst, recently discharged from the service, was a player of unusual versatility. Originally a shortstop, he played the outfield for the Cardinals in 1945, then switched over to second base the next year. In 1945, the rookie batted .278 and led the league with 26 stolen bases.

All of the stars were back from the war in 1946 and the game prospered as never before. Five of the eight National League teams, including the

116

Debs Garms, who gave the Cardinals some games in the outfield and at third base from 1943 to 1945.

There were, inevitably, many changes in baseball in 1946, including in St. Louis. After six remarkably successful seasons, Southworth decided to accept a lucrative offer to manage the Boston Braves. His replacement was another man from the organization, Eddie Dyer. The forty-five-year-old Dyer had been a left-handed pitcher with the Redbirds back in the 1920s, pitching with little distinction and then leaving the big leagues with a sore arm in 1927. Thereafter he had served in the organization in various managerial and executive capacities, including head of the farm system, before being elevated to skipper of the big club.

Joe Garagiola (1946–51). He always made fun of his hitting, but his lifetime average was a modestly respectable .257.

Cardinals, set new attendance records. With 1,061,807 cash customers, the Redbirds exceeded their previous high by 300,000. Helping to build this total was a blistering pennant race as the Cardinals and Dodgers picked up where they had left off in 1942, this time fighting down to the first deadlock in baseball history—each team finished the season with identical 96–58 records.

The great Cardinal outfield in 1946. *Left to right:* Stan Musial, Terry Moore, and Enos Slaughter.

Back in Redbird uniforms were Stan Musial, Enos Slaughter, Terry Moore, Harry Walker, Howie Pollett, Walker Cooper, Murry Dickson, Al Brazle, Johnny Beazley, Max Lanier, Ernie White, and others. While some of them played up to or beyond their prewar capacities, others did not. Beazley had injured his arm during the war and was of little help. Another sore-armed pitcher, White, was sold to Boston early in the season. And even before the season opened, the club sold its catcher, Cooper, to the Giants for $175,000. Cooper was replaced behind the plate by a tandem of Del Rice and a witty, congenial twenty-year-old named Joe Garagiola. Joe would later make a second career as TV personality and baseball announcer, trading humorously on his weak hitting; but in September he smashed a crucial three-run homer against the Dodgers that gave the

Cardinals one of the many "must-win" games they played during a pulsating stretch run.

The club suffered a heavy blow early in the season. In Mexico, the money-laden Pasquel brothers were launching what proved to be a short-lived enterprise called the Mexican League, an effort to bring big-time baseball to their country. For credibility, they needed big leaguers, and the inducement was that old, reliable temptation—money.

Because Breadon was notorious for paying low salaries, the Cardinals were one of the Pasquels' targeted clubs. Musial was courted, but resisted a pile of cash that was placed before him on his kitchen table, loyalty and common sense being part of the star's arsenal of virtues. Three of his teammates, however, yielded—Lanier, second baseman Lou Klein, and pitcher Freddie Martin. (A few "name" players suc-

(ABOVE) *Left:* Second baseman Lou Klein (1943, 1945–46, 1949), who went south of the border in 1946. *Middle:* Right-hander Freddie Martin (1946, 1949–50), who joined Klein and Lanier in their jump to the Mexican League. *Right:* Max Lanier with the Vera Cruz team in the Mexican League. "I couldn't believe," Max said, "there was that much difference between two countries that were so close together."

cumbed to the blandishments from south of the border, most prominent among them Giants relief star Ace Adams and Brooklyn catcher Mickey Owen and outfielder Luis Olmo—and the men from St. Louis.)

The defections took place in May and Lanier's in particular was painful, for Max had begun the season in blazing style—six starts, six complete games, six victories, and a 1.93 ERA. All of the jumpers were immediately hit with five-year suspensions from organized ball by Commissioner Happy Chandler. The Mexican League soon collapsed and the suspensions were eventually modified and in 1949 the defectors were allowed to return to baseball.

As had been the case in 1942, the Dodgers dissipated a comfortable lead in 1946, this time a

7½ -game advantage in early July. The race went on through a scorching hot summer and into September. Baseball, which prides itself on a season whose length was designed to determine the best team, found out that not even its protracted schedule was always enough to raise a winner. On the season's final day, St. Louis and Brooklyn were tied for first place. The Cardinals were beaten by the Cubs, 8–3, but an old friend pulled their spuds out of the fire—pitching for the Braves, Mort Cooper pitched a masterful 4–0 shutout of the Dodgers, forcing a St. Louis–Brooklyn playoff.

National League rules called for a best-of-three playoff (in the American League it was one sudden-death game). This first-ever shoot-out opened in St. Louis, where Pollett beat the

Left to right: Manager Eddie Dyer, Stan Musial, Enos Slaughter, and Whitey Kurowski. They're at Brooklyn's Ebbets Field in September 1946.

Dodgers, 4–2. The second game, in Brooklyn, saw the Cardinals build up an 8–1 lead, then have to perspire through a valiant ninth-inning Dodger rally. The Brooks scored three runs and had the bases loaded when Brecheen, in relief of Dickson, fanned Eddie Stanky and Howie Schultz and sent another pennant into the skies of St. Louis. For Brecheen, it was the beginning of what was going to be a red-hot roll.

The Cardinals' ninth pennant was won, once more, by a team that had come almost entirely from the farm system. Musial, playing most of the season at first base, had a blazing year, leading in batting (.365), hits (228), doubles (50), triples (20), runs (124), slugging (.587), and total bases (366). He was an easy winner of his second MVP Award.

Schoendienst was now established at second base, Marion continued to write the book at shortstop, and Kurowksi completed the infield. Terry Moore, at thirty-four the team's oldest player, was flanked in center by Harry Walker and Enos ("Country") Slaughter. Enos, smarting whenever they walked Musial to get at him

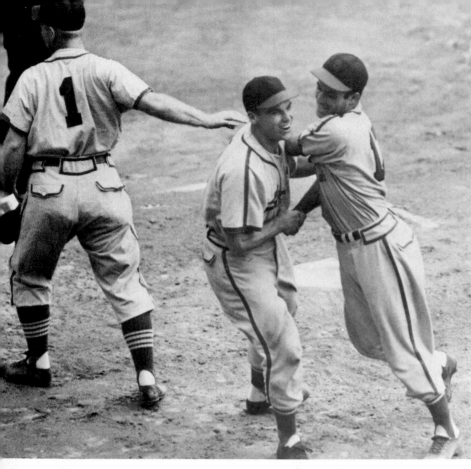

Joe Garagiola being greeted at home plate by Whitey Kurowski (No. 1) and Dick Sisler (*center*) after hitting a big three-run homer against the Dodgers at Ebbets Field.

Four Cardinal southpaws. *Left to right:* Al Brazle, Howie Pollett, Max Lanier, and Harry Brecheen.

Sylvester ("Blix") Donnelly (1944–46), who turned in some snappy relief work for the Cardinals during the war.

Manager Eddie Dyer sits disconsolately in the Cardinals clubhouse September 29, 1946, after the Redbirds lost 8–3 to the Cubs.

St. Louis wins the pennant on October 3, 1946, as Harry Brecheen strikes out Brooklyn's Howie Schultz in the bottom of the ninth inning with two outs and the bases loaded. The playoff game was played at Ebbets Field in Brooklyn.

Stan Musial selecting some lumber. He usually found the right one.

Stan "The Man" bringing home the bacon as the ball eludes catcher Ernie Lombardi.

One of the great keystone tandems in Cardinal history: Red Schoendienst *(left)* and Marty Marion.

("It only made me more determined," he said), batted .300 and led the league with 130 RBIs. Garagiola and Rice handled the catching.

Pollett was 21-10, leading the league in victories and ERA (2.10), followed by Dickson (15-6) and Brecheen (15-15), with some sharp bullpen work from Brazle and Wilks. The team had the best marks in batting, fielding, and earned run average, fulfilling anybody's definition of balance.

The Boston Red Sox had torn through the American League and run away with their first pennant in 28 years. Joe Cronin's club featured the mighty bat of Ted Williams, abetted by the solid punch of Bobby Doerr, Johnny Pesky, Rudy York, and Dominic DiMaggio. Cronin

St. Louis's wonderful center fielder, Terry Moore (1935-42, 1946-48).

Harry ("The Hat") Walker (1940–43, 1946–47, 1950–51, 1955), fussing with his cap. Harry managed the Redbirds in 1955.

Enos Slaughter, who set the standard for hustle.

son. The club's 20 hits tied a Series record, with the attack being highlighted by Slaughter, Kurowski, and Garagiola, each of whom had four hits.

The Red Sox won the fifth game behind Dobson, 6–3, as an ailing Pollett gave way in the first inning to Brazle. So it was a confident Boston team that entrained with the Cardinals for St. Louis to decide the championship. Adding to the Cardinal woes was the damaged elbow of Enos Slaughter, who had been struck by an errant Dobson pitch in Game 5. Unable to throw or to swing a bat, Slaughter had to ask to be removed from the game, leading one writer to observe, "If Enos Slaughter asks to be taken out of the lineup he has to be near death." Well, it wasn't that serious, but it was bad enough. Slaughter was warned that an-

Howie Pollett (1941–43, 1946–51). The classy lefty was a twenty-game winner in 1946 and 1949.

also had quality pitchers in right-handers Dave Ferriss and Tex Hughson (both twenty-game winners), Joe Dobson, and southpaw Mickey Harris. It promised to be an exciting World Series and it was, climaxed by a daring "mad dash" around the bases that has forever epitomized the Cardinal style of play.

The Series opened in St. Louis with Boston beating Pollett in ten innings, 3–2. The next day the screwballing Brecheen began putting his stamp on things with a 3–0 shutout.

Moving to Fenway Park, the Cardinals found themselves stymied in Game 3 by Ferriss, who defeated Dickson, 4–0. The Cardinals exploded in Game 4 with 20 hits and a 12–3 victory behind George Munger, who had been discharged from the military in midsea-

Righty Murry Dickson (1939–40, 1942–43, 1946–48, 1956–57). His top year with the Cardinals was 15–6 in 1946.

It's the first inning of Game 2 of the 1946 World Series. Boston's Tom McBride is out at second on the front end of a double play. Red Schoendienst is watching Marty Marion's peg to first base. Making the call is umpire Charlie Berry.

Harry Brecheen (1940, 1943–52). They called him "The Cat."

other blow on the elbow could end his career, but the gritty symbol of Cardinal hustle said, "I guess I'll have to take that gamble."

Brecheen kept the Cardinals alive with a 4–1 victory in Game 6, leaving the stage lit for a seventh game. "The seventh game of the World Series," Slaughter said years later in reminiscence. "Say it aloud—it's got a *sound* to it, doesn't it?" The game turned out to more than justify its dramatic rank in the mythos of baseball.

With Dickson on the mound, St. Louis took a 3–1 lead into the top of the eighth. The Red Sox then rallied for two runs to tie it, knocking out Dickson. The man summoned by Eddie Dyer to shut down the Sox was Brecheen, who had already won two games in the Series.

Slaughter led off the inning with a single, then remained in place as the next two batters were retired. With Harry Walker at bat, Enos took off to steal second.

Years later, in the tranquillity of recollection, Slaughter spoke of the moment, his moment in baseball history, when the North Carolina farmboy who had always run hard, as a youngster, as a minor leaguer, as a major league star, until he had finally become the archetypal St. Louis Cardinal, his speed and hustle and daring virtually an organization symbol as much as that pair of proud redbirds, made a now legendary nonstop circuit of the bases, with a World Championship in suspension and waiting to be taken.

"Harry hit one into left center," Slaughter said, "not too hard. I had got a good jump and when I got to second and saw where the ball was going I said to myself, 'I can score.' I kept going. I never broke stride. I had it in my head that I was going to score. Sometimes you just make up your mind about something and everything else gets locked out. I still don't know to this day if our third-base coach Mike Gonzales ever gave me the stop sign or not. It wouldn't have made a lick of difference if he'd had. I rounded third and kept going. When I got ready to slide into home I saw Roy Partee, the catcher, take about two or three steps up in front of the plate and I slid across easily."

No moment of baseball legend is complete without some adjunct, and this one was no different. Walker's softly tapped base hit was picked up in left-center and fired to shortstop Johnny Pesky, who naturally had his back to the infield as he received the relay. Second baseman Bobby Doerr, with the play in front of him, shouted to Johnny to go home with the ball, but with more than 36,000 Cardinal fans up on their feet yelling, Doerr's voice was like vespers in a hurricane. Pesky didn't know where Slaughter was and when he turned around the Boston shortstop hesitated for a split

George Munger (1943–44, 1946–52). He was 16–5 in 1947.

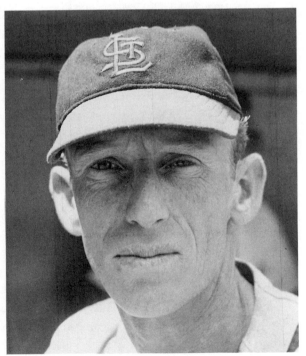

Left-hander Al Brazle (1943, 1946–54), who gave the Cardinals years of excellent relief pitching.

Enos Slaughter completing his famous "mad dash" around the bases in the eighth inning of Game 7 of the 1946 World Series. Red Sox catcher Roy Partee has gone up the line for the peg. Watching are Marty Marion and umpire Al Barlick.

second before throwing home. Whether or not the slight hesitation allowed Slaughter to score remains a fair subject for debate. When it did come, Pesky's throw was not only late but up the line. Enos slid home easily.

"I guess I'll always be remembered for that more than for anything else," Slaughter said, "and that's just fine with me, because it was right in my style of play."

In the top of the ninth, the Red Sox put runners on first and third with one out, but Brecheen extricated himself from the situation and held on for a 4–3 victory, giving the Cardinals their sixth World Championship.

The '46 World Series remains a dramatic high point in Cardinal history. The club had taken four pennants and three championships in five years and had assumed, by baseball standards, dynastic status. But for Cardinal fans, the game-winning dust thrown up by Slaughter's memorable, all-cylinders rush home was going to have to remain in the air for a long time, for it would be 18 years before their team again saw the inside of a World Series.

BETWEEN PENNANTS

B Y 1947 THERE WAS ANOTHER dynasty moving into place in the National League: the Brooklyn Dodgers, meticulously and boldly put together by Branch Rickey—meticulously because of Rickey's successful farm system; boldly because of his revolutionary move in signing black players, the first of whom was Jackie Robinson, who galvanized the Dodgers to the pennant in 1947. From 1947 through 1956, the Dodgers won six pennants, with the other four going to the New York Giants, Boston Braves (managed by Billy Southworth), and Philadelphia Phillies—a ten-year dominance by the four Eastern clubs.

Like most National (and American) League clubs, the Cardinals were slow in enlisting black talent—first baseman Tom Alston in 1954 being their first. In addition, the rich ore they had been mining in their farm system began to peter out. The postwar prosperity had brought changes, among them the bonus player. The talent nets that the Cardinals had always swept across the sandlots of America were bringing in ever-lighter catches as more and more of the talented youngsters were holding out for, and receiving, large signing bonuses.

The world champions stumbled badly early in the 1947 season, losing 11 of their first 13, and though a midseason drive brought them to within 3½ games of the Dodgers in the middle of July, they never got any closer, finishing second, five games behind.

Part of the problem in 1947 was an attack of appendicitis suffered by Musial early in the season that so weakened him his average was under .200 for weeks. A murderous second-half surge enabled The Man to finish at .312, his lowest average between 1942 and 1956. An aching back held Pollett to a 9–11 record. The ace's role this year was assumed by George Munger (16–5); World Series hero Brecheen was 16–11. Whitey Kurowski had his best

Outfielder Erv Dusak (1941–42, 1946–51). Hitting some key home runs earned him the nickname "Four Sack."

Outfielder–first baseman Dick Sisler (1946–47, 1952–53).

season, batting .310, driving in 104 runs, and hitting 27 home runs, 12 of them in August, which set a one-month home run record for the club. It was Whitey's last big season; injuries held him to 77 games the next year and by 1949 he was through, just thirty years old.

The Cardinals also hurt themselves with an early-season trade when they sent Harry Walker to the Phillies for power-hitting outfielder Ron Northey. While Northey hit adequately for St. Louis during the next few seasons, Walker turned in the year of his life,

Del Rice (1945–55, 1960), longtime Cardinal catcher.

Jim Hearn (1947–50). This big right-hander was 12–7 in 1947; the Cardinals later gave up on him and he went on to have some fine seasons with the New York Giants.

going on to lead the league with a .363 average, the only National Leaguer ever to win a batting championship while playing on two different clubs.

Despite all, the team went on to set a new St. Louis attendance record with 1,247,913 spins of the turnstiles.

Fittingly, with the end of the greatest run of success in the club's history, the Sam Breadon era came to an end. The longtime owner of the Cardinals was seventy-one years old now and his health had begun to fail (cancer took his life in 1949). Historically, it was probably a good time for Sam to get out of the game. Notably parsimonious (he once ordered an office clock

Manager Eddie Dyer (*seated, left*) has plenty of company as he pockets the contract he just signed to manage the Cardinals in 1948. Sam Breadon is seated behind the desk. Standing (*left to right*) are Harry Brecheen, Whitey Kurowski, Enos Slaughter, Terry Moore, Ron Northey, and Howie Pollett.

A quintet of Cardinal pitchers gathers for a photo session during spring training, 1948. *Left to right:*
Howie Pollett, George Munger, Murry Dickson, Harry Brecheen, and Ken Burkhart.

unplugged to save on electricity), it is unlikely he would have tried to attract talented youngsters to St. Louis with tempting bonuses. And the farm system now had more arid patches than fertile ones. The world in which Sam Breadon had been comfortable and successful was passing.

The new owners of the Cardinals were Fred Saigh and Robert Hannegan. Saigh (the name was pronounced "sigh") was a St. Louis lawyer who had done well in real estate. Hannegan was a St. Louis native whose father had been the city's chief of police. A gregarious character with a big smile and firm handshake, Hannegan, also a lawyer, augmented an already sizable income with a series of successful commercial investments. He later became active in Democratic politics and in January 1944 became chairman of the Democratic National Committee (from which position he

helped Missouri senator Harry Truman win the party's vice-presidential nomination), and later Postmaster General. When he joined with Saigh to buy the Cardinals, Hannegan resigned his cabinet post. Plagued by ill health, he sold out to Saigh a little over a year later. Not long after, in October 1949, he died at the age of 46.

The Cardinals gave their new owners a second-place slot in 1948, finishing 6½ games behind the Braves. The 1948 season saw Stan Musial at his absolute peak. In winning his third MVP Award, the twenty-seven-year-old star won his third batting crown with a career-high .376 average, as well as leading in hits (230, which was 40 more than the runner-up), doubles (46), triples (18), runs (135), RBIs (131), total bases (429), and slugging (.702). The total base and slugging figures remain the league's highest by any player since 1930. Musial's 39 home runs left him one short of tying for the

Those Redbird victory smiles belong to *(left to right)*, Enos Slaughter, Ted Wilks, Eddie Dyer, and Stan Musial.

lead with Johnny Mize and Ralph Kiner and thus deprived him of the Triple Crown, the one batting jewel that was to elude him.

It was during the 1948 season that Pittsburgh outfielder Wally Westlake, after hammering the ball in batting practice, stepped out of the cage, encountered Musial, and said, "Stan, I feel like I'm gonna get four hits today. You ever have that feeling?"

"Every day," Musial said.

And on some days he was even better than that. On April 30, May 19, June 22, and September 22, the Cardinals' methodical manufacturer of base hits tied Ty Cobb's modern record by connecting for five hits in a game four times in a single season.

It was also a banner year for Harry Brecheen. The slender southpaw, whose feline features earned him the nickname "The Cat," was 20–7, leading the league in strikeouts (149), shutouts (7), and ERA (2.24).

Fred Saigh *(left)* and Bob Hannegan.

This did happen now and then: Stan Musial popping up. The catcher is Brooklyn's Bruce Edwards.

Stan Musial (*left*) with young first baseman Vernal ("Nippy") Jones (1946–51), who was a .300 hitter in 1948.

Harry Brecheen.

The Cardinals registered a third straight second-place finish in 1949, losing by a single game. The exciting summer-long race generated a new club attendance record—1,430,676—which would stand until 1966.

Dyer's men were in the race until the season's final day, when Brooklyn, with a one-game lead, defeated the Phillies in ten innings to clinch the pennant. A four-game losing streak in the season's closing week cost the Redbirds dearly. Some people felt, however, that the team had lost the pennant the preceding January, when they sold Murry Dickson to Pittsburgh for $125,000. The veteran right-

Tommy Glaviano is safe at home as Brooklyn backstop Bruce Edwards blocks the plate but misses the tag. The umpire is Dusty Boggess. Tommy served the Cardinals in a utility role from 1949 through 1952.

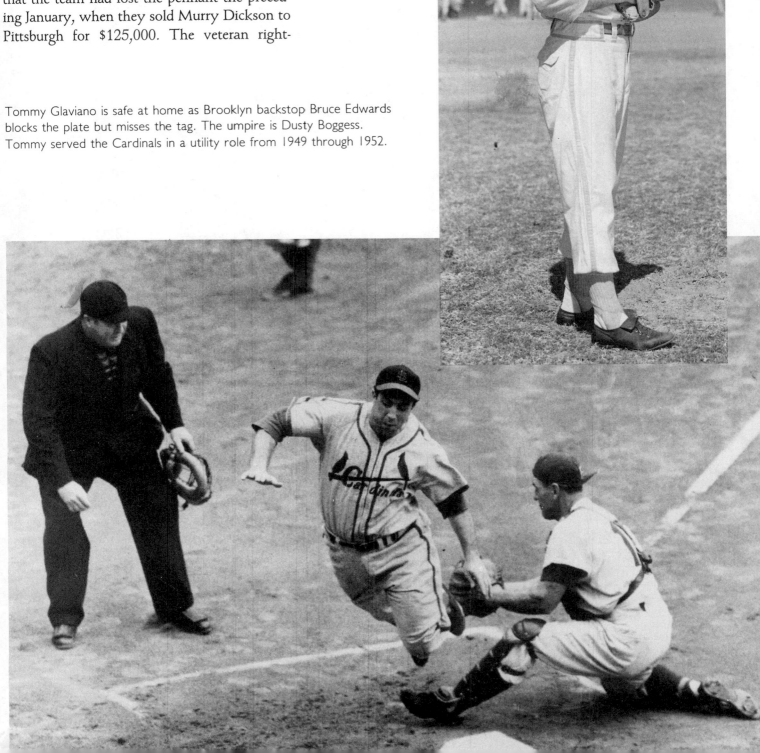

An aerial view of Sportsman's Park in the 1950s.

hander plagued his former teammates all season, beating them five times.

Even without Dickson, the St. Louis pitching was strong, with Pollett resuming his role as ace with a 20–9 record, Munger going 15–8, and four others winning in double figures, including right-hander Gerry Staley (10–10), soon to become the staff leader. Ted Wilks was 10–3 in relief, appearing in 59 games. The Cardinal pitchers led the league with a 3.44 ERA, but couldn't match Brooklyn's all-around play: the Dodgers led the league with 152 home runs to 102 for St. Louis, 117 stolen bases to a mere 17 for St. Louis, and made the fewest errors.

Musial batted .338 (losing the title by four points to Jackie Robinson), again led in hits (207), doubles (41), triples (13), and total bases (383), while Slaughter hit a career-high .336.

It had been a tough, exciting race, reminiscent of the classic long-span duels with Brooklyn in 1941, 1942, and 1946, and it closed out the club's high-water decade, during which they finished first four times, second five times, and third once. The memories would have to keep them warm during the long winter of the 1950s.

In 1950 the Cardinals dropped to fifth place, the first time since 1938 they ended in the second division and the first time since 1940 that

Former Yankee Johnny Lindell (second from right) is being greeted upon joining the Cardinals in 1950. The committee consists of Eddie Dyer (left), Stan Musial, and Enos Slaughter.

they hadn't been first or second. With many of the bright young rookies of yesterday beginning to give way to age or injury, Stan Musial remained the glory of St. Louis, winning his fourth batting championship with a .346 average and his fifth slugging title (.596). He was the team's only .300 hitter, though Schoendienst led the league with 43 doubles.

The 1950 season marked the end of Eddie Dyer's five-year tenure as manager. In 1951 the new skipper, something of a surprise, was Marty Marion, the club's thirty-three-year-old

The sweet swing of Stan Musial.

Right-hander Gerry Staley (1947–54). He was a 19-game winner in 1951.

Wally Westlake in a June 15 deal that saw Garagiola, Wilks, and Pollett leave the Cardinals.

On December 11, another trade brought St. Louis its new manager. The man that Saigh wanted was Giants second baseman Eddie Stanky, now thirty-five years old and with his playing career winding down. To get Eddie from New York, St. Louis sent Lanier and out-fielder Chuck Diering.

Stanky had played for Leo Durocher in Brooklyn and New York and was in some respects a Durocher clone: Eddie was a sound baseball man who had a knack for irritating the opposition as well as the umpires, whom he sometimes seemed to number among the opposition. It was Stanky the player who had been famously evaluated by Branch Rickey: "He can't run, he can't throw, he can't hit. He can only beat you." This was a tribute to Ed-

shortstop, whose playing career had ended prematurely because of a back injury.

Marion lasted just one year in the job, bringing the club in third, well behind the Dodgers and Giants, whose red-hot September race culminated in Bobby Thomson's famous ninth-inning playoff-game home run.

The Cardinals and Stan Musial continued to be synonymous. In 1951, Musial became the first National Leaguer since Hornsby in the 1920s to repeat as batting champion, this time with a .355 average. His 12 triples gave him the lead for the fifth time, a new league record.

Gerry Staley led the pitching staff with a 19–13 record, followed by 11-game winners Max Lanier (reinstated after his Mexican adventure) and Cliff Chambers. Chambers had come to St. Louis from Pittsburgh along with

Southpaw Cliff Chambers (1951–53).

Eddie Stanky, who managed the Cardinals from 1952 to 1955. Eddie put in some time at second base in 1952–53.

Cloyd Boyer (1949–52), the oldest of the three Boyer brothers who made it to the majors. Possessor of a live fastball, Cloyd's career was ended by an arm injury.

Red Schoendienst, star second baseman and future Cardinal manager.

Enos Slaughter (*right*) and rookie right-hander Stu Miller in 1952. A crafty pitcher who did much of his work in relief, Miller was with the Cardinals from 1952 to 1956. It was said that he had three pitches—slow, slower, and slowest.

Shortstop and future manager Solly Hemus (1949–56, 1959).

die's spirit, aggressiveness, and shrewd baseball sense, all of which Eddie came charging into St. Louis to impart. (Later in the 1952 season, the departed Marion resurfaced as manager of the Browns, replacing another former Cardinal icon, Rogers Hornsby.)

The 1952 edition put together the best record of any Cardinal team of the decade—88–66, finishing third, 8½ games behind Brooklyn. The game of the year for St. Louis occurred at New York's Polo Grounds on June 15. After four innings, the Redbirds were losing to the Giants 11–0. If this weren't sufficiently disheartening, the Giants had their ace pitcher, Sal Maglie, on the mound. In addition the Cardinals also had precedent against them—no club in league history had ever overcome an

Stan Musial receiving a silver bat emblematic of the batting title he won in 1952. Making the presentation is National League President Warren Giles.

Right-hander Eddie Yuhas (1952–53), who gave the Cardinals one year of superb relief work before going under with an arm injury.

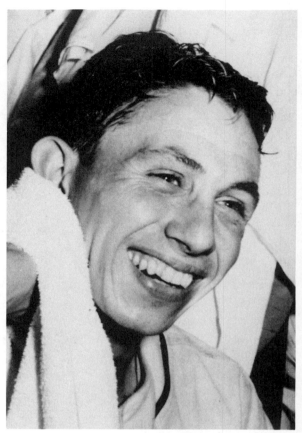

Harvey Haddix (1953–56), who broke in as a 20-game winner.

11-run deficit and gone on to win. But the Cardinals scored seven in the top of the fifth, three in the seventh, and two each in the eighth and ninth and went on to a 14–12 win.

The '52 Cardinals topped the league with a .267 batting average, led by Musial, whose .336 mark gave him his third straight batting crown and sixth overall. He also led in slugging for the sixth time (.538), hits (194) for the sixth time, doubles (42) for the fifth time, and total bases (311) for the sixth time. Slaughter and Schoendienst were also .300 hitters and Staley led the staff with a 17–14 record. The club had one of the best right-left bullpen tandems in its history that year in rookie right-hander Eddie Yuhas and southpaw Al Brazle. Yuhas was 12–2 with a 2.73 ERA and Brazle 12–5 and 2.72. Unfortunately, Eddie's career was scrubbed by a sore arm the following spring.

Meanwhile new ownership was on its way to the Cardinals. Clubowner Fred Saigh had run afoul of the Internal Revenue Service on income-tax charges and, during the 1952 season, was socked with a fine and a fifteen-month jail sentence. Realizing he had become an embarrassment to baseball, Saigh reluctantly agreed to sell his team.

The new owner of the Cardinals was the Anheuser-Busch Brewery, which was the same as saying August Anheuser Busch, Jr., known informally as "Gussie." A character as flavorsome as his beechwood-aged product, Busch was popular and well-liked, one who enjoyed the accouterments of good living, which included riding show horses and riding to the hounds. He was a baron of mid-America, born with a strong competitive streak and a desire to excel, be it among the brewmasters or—as was now the case—the ball clubs of the National League.

After the 1953 season (in which the Cardinals finished in a tie for third place), Busch suddenly found himself the sole proprietor of major league baseball in St. Louis. Bill Veeck, operating the Browns with laughs, jokes, promotions, and frayed shoestrings, had been hoping Saigh would move the Cardinal franchise to another city. When Busch bought the team, however, that hope evaporated and it was Veeck who was now looking to go elsewhere. Suffocating under declining attendance (in 1953, the Browns drew fewer than 300,000), Veeck desperately needed a location. He decided on Baltimore. But Veeck's freewheeling personality and gimmicky ideas and promotions (it was he who had employed midget Eddie Gaedel as a pinch-hitter) had long been irritating his fellow owners, whose permission was needed in order for him to relocate. This fraternity regarded Veeck as kindly as they would have a tight shoe and used the opportunity to rid themselves of him by denying the needed permission; Veeck had to sell out. His divestments included Sportsman's Park, which was ultimately sold to Anheuser-Busch, who promptly renamed the old ball yard Busch Stadium and appropriately so, for Gussie had spent over $2 million in renovating it.

The third-place Cardinals were buoyed by some sterling personal achievements in 1953: Schoendienst batted a career-high .342 and Musial came in at .337, with a league-leading 53 doubles. Though Schoendienst lost the batting title to Brooklyn's Carl Furillo by two points, he did accomplish something notable—he was the first Cardinal since 1942 to outhit Musial, his roommate and close friend.

For fifteen years the Cardinals had been bringing up quality left-handed pitching—Lanier, Pollett, White, Brecheen, Brazle—and now they added another in rookie Harvey Haddix. Nicknamed "The Kitten" (he was now the club's lone feline, as Harry The Cat was wrapping up his career with the Browns in 1953), Haddix broke in with what was to be the best record of his 14-year career: 20-9 and a league-high six shutouts.

Stan Musial (*left*) and former Yankee third baseman Billy Johnson (1951–53).

Ray Jablonski (1953–54, 1959).

The club also received a fine season from another rookie, third baseman Ray Jablonski. "Jabbo" hit 21 home runs (a club record for rookies) and drove in 112 runs. The former Red Sox farmhand was a solid hitter, but he carried some heavy baggage—limited range afield and a sometimes recalcitrant glove. He made 27 errors and posted the lowest fielding average of any third baseman in the league at .932.

Just before the opening of the 1954 season, the Cardinals ended Enos Slaughter's 20-year affiliation with the organization by trading their veteran symbol of hustle and desire to the Yankees for several minor leaguers.

"It cut my heart out," Slaughter said. "I cried

A gathering of Redbird pitchers in spring training, 1953. *Left to right:* Harvey Haddix, Stu Miller, Gerry Staley, Cliff Chambers, and Wilmer ("Vinegar Bend") Mizell.

Enos Slaughter shortly after being told he was no longer a Cardinal.

like a baby. I couldn't help it. I'd been a Cardinal since 1935, and I don't think anybody who's ever worn a Cardinal uniform was ever more loyal to it than I was or put out as hard as I did or gave as much. But you go. Of course you go. You have to."

The 1954 Cardinals reaffirmed once again— if anyone ever doubted it—that pitching was the cornerstone of success when they led the league in batting (.281) and runs (799) and yet finished in only sixth place. Musial, Schoendienst, catcher Bill Sarni, and Rookie of the Year outfielder Wally Moon all batted over .300. The club also received good hitting from Jablonski, young first baseman Joe Cunning-

Over his career Stan Musial scored 1,949 runs. Here is one of them, being registered at New York's Polo Grounds in June 1953. Wes Westrum is the catcher, No. 11 is Ray Jablonski, and Jocko Conlon is the umpire.

(TOP LEFT) Wally Moon (1954–58), the 1954 National League Rookie of the Year.

(TOP RIGHT) Outfielder Rip Repulski (1953–56). He hit 23 homers in 1955.

Joe Presko (1951–54). Injuries aborted the right-hander's career.

Tom Poholsky (1950–51, 1954–56). The best the tall righty could do was nine victories in a season.

(TOP RIGHT) Outfielder Harry ("Peanuts") Lowery (1950–54). The veteran led the league in pinch hits with 13 in 1952 and 22 in 1953.

(BOTTOM RIGHT) Former Yankee ace Vic Raschi (1954–55), who coughed up Hank Aaron's first major league home run.

ham, and outfielder Rip Repulski. The club seemed to be able to reach out blindfolded and find a hitter. Pitching was another matter.

Haddix turned in a fine sophomore year at 18–13 and Brooks Lawrence, a twenty-nine-year-old rookie right-hander, was 15–6. No one else won more than eight, and that eight-game winner was one-time New York Yankee ace Vic Raschi, obtained in a cash transaction.

147

(ABOVE LEFT) The National League's 1955 Rookie of the Year, Bill Virdon (1955–56).

(ABOVE RIGHT) Ken Boyer (1955–56), the top third baseman in Cardinal history. His 255 homers are second only to Musial's 475 on the club ledger. Boyer managed the Redbirds from 1978 to 1980.

Brooks Lawrence (1954–55), who broke in with a fine 15–6 record in 1955. After going 3–8 the next year, he was traded to the Reds.

Raschi's most memorable moment in a Cardinal uniform was not a positive one—on April 23 he served up the first of Hank Aaron's 755 major league home runs.

"I showed him how to do it," Raschi said wryly, years later. When the intensely competitive right-hander was asked how he would have felt had he known the blow would one day be considered historic, he said, "I would have been just as ticked off. It wasn't historic for me."

While Aaron's pursuit of home run history would take two decades to complete, Stan Musial made some long-ball history of his own in one day, on May 2, 1954. In a doubleheader against the Giants at Busch Stadium, The Man, never known as a home-run hitter in the classic sense, set a new major league record (tied by San Diego's Nate Colbert in 1972) by hitting five of them, three in the first game, two in the second. This was from a man who said he never swung for the fences, although he conceded later that in his final at bat that day he was trying for number 6. He popped out.

"It goes to show you," Musial said.

The team's 72–82 record in 1954 was their first sub-.500 mark since 1938, and a year later things got worse. The Redbirds spun out of control to a 68–86 mark and seventh-place finish, their worst since 1919. Stanky was fired after 36 games, replaced by former Cardinal outfielder Harry Walker, then in his fourth year as manager of the Rochester farm club. Known as "The Hat" during his playing days because of his habit of fidgeting with his cap while at bat, Walker's specialty was hitting and for years after his retirement from organized ball he remained a guru to whom struggling big league hitters were often sent for some tutoring.

Despite their seventh-place finish in 1955, the Cardinals that year set a club home-run record that still stands—143, led by Musial's 33 dingers. They also produced the Rookie of the Year for the second year in a row in outfielder Bill Virdon. A .281 hitter, Virdon had come to St. Louis from the Yankees in the Slaughter deal. Another rookie was Ken Boyer, a twenty-

Frank Lane, the Cardinals' colorful general manager.

four-year-old third baseman with a power bat, sure glove, and strong arm. Ken's older brother Cloyd had pitched for the Cardinals a few years earlier, but a sore arm had aborted the career of the promising fastballer. Ken's younger brother Clete was an eighteen-year-old bonus player with the Kansas City Athletics that year, with a long career with the Yankees and Braves ahead of him. But the best of the talented Boyers was Ken, destined to become the greatest third baseman in Cardinal history. In his break-in season, Boyer batted .264 and hit 18 home runs.

In October 1955, the Cardinals hired Frank Lane as general manager. Lane was a gregarious baseball lifer, noted for the alacrity with which he made trades, some of which seemed to be made just for the sake of making them. Lane's insistence on doing things his way—his sometimes impulsive, occasionally questionable way—made it almost a certainty that he wouldn't last too long in any job, and indeed during his long career he worked for at least eight major league clubs, in one capacity or an-

A quartet of brand-new Redbirds. Acquired in a June 14, 1956, trade with the New York Giants are, *(left to right)*, outfielder Whitey Lockman (1956), catcher Ray Katt (1956, 1958–59), southpaw Don Liddle (1956), and shortstop Alvin Dark (1956–58).

other. His most famous caper occurred in 1957 when as the Cleveland Indians' GM he swapped managers—Joe Gordon to Detroit for Jimmy Dykes.

Lane's energetic new broom lasted only two years in St. Louis. A report that Frank was prepared to trade Stan Musial to the Phillies for ace right-hander Robin Roberts alerted August

Bill Sarni (1951–52, 1954–56). Bill was a .300 hitter in 1954. Traded to the New York Giants in 1956, he suffered a heart attack shortly after that, which ended his playing career.

Manager Fred Hutchinson *(center)* with, *(left)*, Whitey Lockman and right-hander Herman Wehmeier (1956–58).

Busch that perhaps his GM had a bit too much autonomy and virtually assured that his St. Louis would soon become but another entry on Lane's résumé.

While he was in office, Lane did swap the Cardinals' second most popular player, Red Schoendienst. Red went to the Giants on June 14, 1956, as part of an eight-player deal that brought to St. Louis shortstop Alvin Dark, outfielder Whitey Lockman, catcher Ray Kaat, and left-hander Don Liddle. Along with Schoendienst went catcher Bill Sarni and pitchers Gordon Jones and Dick Littlefield. The trade did not go down very well with St. Louis fans, particularly when none of the new men contributed very much to the local cause. (The Giants soon traded Schoendienst to Milwaukee, where he went on to help the Braves to two pennants.)

For Harry Walker, Lane's arrival was a sign to reach for the departure schedules. The new skipper was thirty-seven-year-old Fred Hutchinson, formerly a top right-hander with the Detroit Tigers and for two-and-a-half years their manager. Known as "The Bear," Hutchinson was indeed a bear of a man, big and strong and tough, wired throughout with bristling competitive instincts and easily short-circuited by a temper that in full eruption was one of baseball's glorious spectacles.

"Hutch was a very serious man," one of his players said. "And believe me, we took his seriousness seriously."

Wherever he managed (after leaving the Cardinals he took over the Cincinnati Reds, a job he held for six seasons until stricken by the cancer which took his life in November 1964), Hutchinson had the respect of his players. In

dugout, passing word to his players that he would be in the clubhouse in twenty minutes and expected to find it empty. It was.

Yet, many players attested to a gentle, caring side of Hutchinson.

"Fred had a lot of compassion," one of them said; "he just felt awkward in showing it."

Hutchinson managed the Cardinals for three years, finishing fourth, second, and fifth. The '56 club led the league with a .268 batting average but their top winner was hard-throwing southpaw Wilmer ("Vinegar Bend") Mizell, who was just 14–14. Some people thought the big lefty from Mississippi with the colorful nickname was your prototypical country bumpkin, but after leaving baseball he won a seat in the United States House of Representa-

Hard-throwing left-hander Wilmer ("Vinegar Bend") Mizell (1952–53, 1956–60). His top win total was 14 in 1956.

Shortstop Alex Grammas (1954–56, 1959–62).

some ways, he resembled fellow managers Gil Hodges and Walter Alston, both of whom possessed awesome physical strength and to a certain extent managed by "intimidation," though neither Hodges nor Alston were given to overt demonstrations of temper. Once, while managing Cincinnati, Hutchinson watched his club drop an ill-played doubleheader. After the second game, the seething skipper remained in the

Stan Musial steps in against the Dodgers. The catcher is Brooklyn's Roy Campanella.

tives, from which perch he helped make the annual House-Senate baseball game a strictly no-contest affair.

In 1957, Hutchinson's club was in the middle of a hot pennant race that included the Braves, Dodgers, Phillies, and Reds. As late as the end of July, the fifth-place Redbirds were just 2½ games from the top. The Cardinals were on top in early August, but then suddenly capsized into a nine-game losing streak that dropped them 8½ behind the Braves. A late-season surge brought them to within 2½ of the league penthouse, but then they fell back, finishing second, eight games behind the Braves.

The Cardinals again led the league with a .274 team mark, with Stan Musial scoring a great personal triumph. At the age of thirty-six, the remarkable Redbird took his seventh and final batting title with a .351 average, tying him with Hornsby. (Only Wagner, with eight, has done better in the National League.) The amiable Stanley was like a talisman of baseball's old stability, which was rudely shaken that year by the announcement that the New York Giants and Brooklyn Dodgers would be leaving their ancestral homes for residence in, respectively, San Francisco and Los Angeles, leaving the country's most populated city without National League representation, thus laying the groundwork for expansion.

The Cardinal hitting this year featured ex-Phillies slugger Del Ennis, who drove in 105

Infielder Eddie Kasko (1957–58).

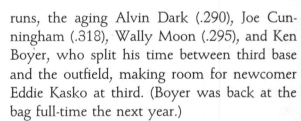

Ken Boyer.

runs, the aging Alvin Dark (.290), Joe Cunningham (.318), Wally Moon (.295), and Ken Boyer, who split his time between third base and the outfield, making room for newcomer Eddie Kasko at third. (Boyer was back at the bag full-time the next year.)

Pitching was the culprit in 1957, with right-handers Larry Jackson and Lindy McDaniel leading the staff with 15–9 records. (McDaniel was soon moved to the bullpen, where he became one of the game's top relievers.) Side-wheeling right-hander Sam Jones, who featured a lethal curve ball, had been acquired from the Cubs in an eight-player Lane spectacular, and was 12–9.

Outfielder Del Ennis (1957–58). This one-time Phillies slugger hit 24 home runs for the Cardinals in 1957 and drove in 105 runs.

The new GM was Vaughan ("Bing") Devine, a St. Louis boy and lifelong Cardinal fan. Devine was as pure a Cardinal front-office man as it was possible to find. He had first hired on in Breadon's office in 1939 as an assistant public relations man. Thereafter, with time out as a Naval officer in World War II, Devine diligently worked his way through the front offices of various Cardinal farm clubs, including the top job at Rochester, before coming to St. Louis as Lane's assistant. One of his early

In a speech at a preseason party, August Busch had said, "If the Cardinals don't win this year or next, Frank Lane will be out on his ass." Everyone laughed. Such stern public warnings are generally regarded as facetious. But the Cardinal boss had not been joking, and after the 1957 season Lane was indeed out, though not on his posterior but on his feet, where Frank usually landed. He took over at Cleveland (where, in one of his first moves, he traded Roger Maris to Kansas City) and the Cardinals had a new general manager.

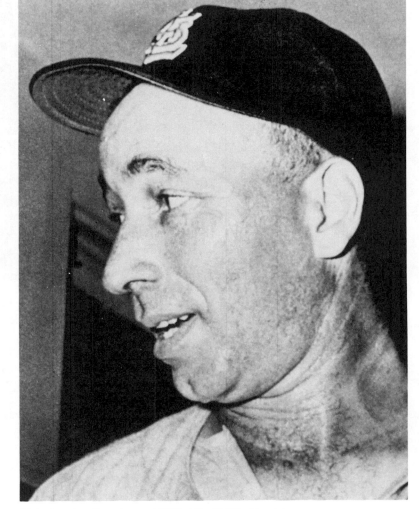

Right-hander Sam Jones (1957–58, 1963). The big sidewheeler was murder on right-handed batters.

The pitching McDaniel brothers, Lindy *(left)* and Von. Lindy (1955–62) won 15 as a starter in 1957, then was converted to a reliever. He pitched in the majors for 21 years. Von was 7–5 as an eighteen-year-old in 1957, then left with a sore arm the following year.

moves as Cardinal GM was a nonmove—canceling a Lane-hatched plan to trade Ken Boyer to Pittsburgh. In all his years in St. Louis, Devine would never make a better decision.

In the spring of 1958 Cardinal fans began preparing themselves for one of baseball's great ceremonial moments—a 3,000th career hit. It was that prodigious hit collector Musial, of course, who was now hot on the trail of that coronating event, which only six players in modern times had achieved: Ty Cobb, Tris Speaker, Honus Wagner, Eddie Collins, Nap Lajoie, and Paul Waner.

Musial had closed the 1957 season with 2,957 hits, 43 short of the elite total he was now in pursuit of. One writer has written:

"Those who played against him in the opening weeks of the 1958 season said they had never seen anything like it. They all knew that Stan Musial was a great hitter—the Cardinal scorcher had been proving it for 15 years—but in the spring of 1958 he was hitting line drives that threatened to start grass fires when they struck the outfield."

Musial tore into National League pitching in the spring of 1958 with pure ferocity. He opened the season with a 17-game hitting streak, during which he batted a stupefying .529. It took him another five games—22 in all—to gather the 43 hits he needed. With 2,999 safe raps in the bank, Musial and the Cardinals were finishing a road trip in Wrigley Field. Hutchinson decided to sit Musial down in order to let Stan smack the big one in St. Louis—

Second baseman Don Blasingame (1955–59).

Right-hander Willard Schmidt (1952–53, 1955–57), used mostly in relief. He was 10–3 in 1957.

"Unless I need him." By the sixth inning of a close game the Cardinals needed him. So Stan came up to pinch-hit and, in front of less than 6,000 Chicago fans, drilled his landmark hit—a run-scoring double, the same as hit No. 1 had been, back in 1941.

Musial's hit was the highlight of a season that saw the Cardinals finish in a tie for fifth place. His .337 average put him over .300 for the 16th consecutive time, a modern league record. Boyer batted .307; otherwise it was an uncharacteristically quiet Redbird lineup, one that finished last in runs scored for the first time in more than 40 years. Sam Jones topped the staff with a 14–13 record and league-leading 225 strikeouts.

The club was struggling, but one harbinger of better days ahead was now in place—twenty-

year-old center fielder Curt Flood, obtained in a steal-of-a-deal with the Reds. The fleet youngster with the magic glove broke in at .261.

Hutchinson was let go at the end of the season, and the new skipper in 1959 was the feisty Solly Hemus, formerly an all-purpose infielder with the team from 1949 to 1955.

Solly ran the club through an undistinguished season in 1959—seventh place—but the glow on the horizon was getting slowly brighter. From the Giants Devine obtained first baseman Bill White (who also played some outfield in the beginning) in exchange for Sam Jones, an excellent long-term trade for St. Louis. White, who in 1989 became president of the National League, was a superb all-around player who was available only because the Giants al-

Stan Musial.

Stan the Man meeting the press after hit number 3,000.

Stan Musial connecting for his 3,000th major league hit against the Cubs at Chicago's Wrigley Field on May 13, 1958. The catcher is Sammy Taylor, the umpire Augie Donatelli.

ready had a logjam around first base with Orlando Cepeda and Willie McCovey. Breaking into a handful of games at the end of the season was the club's future catcher, seventeen-year-old Tim McCarver. And chalking up a 3–5 record in 13 games was twenty-three-year-old right-hander Bob Gibson.

Boyer (.309, 28 homers) and Joe Cunningham (.345) led the attack in 1959, with Kenny putting together a 29-game hitting streak, longest in the league since Musial had a 30-game tear in 1950. For Musial in 1959, it was a precipitous dip to .255, lowest of his career.

"Did they ever boo Musial in St. Louis?" a veteran Cardinal writer was once asked.

"No," the writer said. "They never thought of it. Or if they did, nobody had the guts to be the first."

The Cardinals broke out slowly in 1960, not getting over .500 until early July, then slowly moving into contention. By August 12 they were within three games of first-place Pittsburgh, then lost three straight to the Pirates and never threatened again, finishing in third place, eight games out.

The club was buoyed this year by the strong pitching of sophomore right-hander Ernie Brog-

Solly Hemus, Cardinal manager from 1959 to 1961.

Posing with the big mitts are catchers Hobie Landrith (1957–58) at top, and Hal Smith (1956–61).

On May 15, 1960, the universe of baseball learned that Chicago's Don Cardwell had no-hit the Cardinals, 4–0, and in so doing ended the Cardinals' record 41-year span of not being embarrassed by a no-hitter (their previous stifling had been in 1919), and thus another duly noted event slipped into the archives.

The Cardinals contributed another record-book entry in 1961, one quite the opposite of their notable no-hitting. In consecutive doubleheaders on July 17–18, Bill White tied Ty Cobb's major league record by banging out 14 total hits, eight in the first twin bill, six in the second. (Oddly, when Cobb set his record in 1912, it was on July 17 and 19.)

The '61 Redbirds finished fifth, despite a league-low ERA of 3.74. Along the way they switched managers, with coach Johnny Keane replacing Hemus in midseason. The forty-nine-

lio, who was 21–9, and the veteran Larry Jackson, who was 18–13, while Lindy McDaniel was dazzling in relief, winning 12 and saving 26, earning "greatest relief pitcher I have ever seen" accolades from Hemus.

Julian Javier took over second base and nineteen-year-old left-hander Ray Sadecki broke in with a 9–9 record. Gibson was just 3–6, but already National League hitters were talking about the hurry on his fastball and the bite of his slider.

Rookie right-hander Bob Gibson (1959–75) in 1959.

Catcher Tim McCarver (1959–61, 1963–69, 1973–74), who was a precocious seventeen years old when he broke in. He played in the big leagues for 21 years.

Ken Boyer coming home the hard way against the Milwaukee Braves in 1959. Del Crandall is the catcher, Shag Crawford the umpire.

Right-hander Ernie Broglio (1959–64) and first base-man–outfielder Joe Cunningham (1954, 1956–61). Ernie was a twenty-game winner in 1960, while Joe topped off with a .345 average in 1959.

was to become the top winner among all Car-dinal pitchers had pitched for Keane in the mi-nor leagues and Johnny had developed a profound appreciation of the young man's abil-ities. Gibson himself would later trace his as-cent to stardom to the arrival of Johnny Keane as Cardinal manager in July 1961. Gibson fin-ished the season at 13–12 and would, remark-ably, post consecutively higher winning totals in each of the next five seasons.

In 1962, Keane brought his troops home sixth in what was now a ten-team league, ex-pansion having brought the New York Mets and Houston Colt 45s into the league. Bill White (.324, 104 RBIs) and Ken Boyer (.291, 98 RBIs) did some heavy hitting, but the offen-sive surprise of St. Louis was the now forty-one-year-old Stan Musial. After seasons of .255, .275, and .288, and hearing quiet suggestions

year-old Keane was a lifetime member of the Cardinal organization, as an infielder, minor league manager (for 17 years), and big league coach, and now the soft-spoken, gentlemanly St. Louis native was running the big team.

Keane's first contribution to Cardinal for-tunes was a man-sized one: he put Gibson into the rotation. The Omaha-born fastballer and Hemus had never gotten along. The man who

Larry Jackson (1955–62), a most capable right-handed pitcher for St. Louis. He won 18 games in 1960.

Left to right: first baseman Bill White (1959–65, 1969), catcher Carl Sawatski (1960–63), manager Johnny Keane, and pitcher Larry Jackson.

from various quarters that it might be time for retirement, Musial came back with a .330 season, good for third place in the league. And proving once again that, no matter his age, a great hitter is always potentially lethal, Stan on July 7–8 hit four home runs in consecutive at bats against the New York Mets at the resurrected Polo Grounds, temporary home of the Mets, with the last three homers coming in one game. The feat tied a record and added one more notch in that M-1 of a bat Musial had been firing at National League pitchers since 1941.

Gibson was 15–13, led the team with five shutouts, and struck out 208, the first of nine

seasons in which he would pass the 200 mark in whiffs.

Though they finished six games out in 1963, the Cardinals made an exciting run for the money that year, winning 93 games and coming closer to the top than they had in any season since 1949.

Devine had made a key acquisition when he obtained shortstop Dick Groat, the 1960 MVP, in a deal with Pittsburgh. Groat teamed with White, Javier, and Boyer to give the club one of its finest infields, and also one of its most durable—they averaged 160 games apiece in 1963 and 1964.

The Cardinals were in the race, out of it,

(OPPOSITE TOP) That's Cardinal second baseman Julian Javier firing on to first base to complete a double play. The sliding baserunner is Gus Bell of the New York Mets, while Frank Thomas, who hit the ball, is heading up the line. The action occurred at New York's Polo Grounds in April 1962. Exceptionally gifted with the glove, Javier played for St. Louis from 1960 to 1971.

then back in as the baseball summer of 1963 turned slowly to autumn. They were in first place until early July, lost a three-game series to the Los Angeles Dodgers, and began sputtering. By the end of August they were seven games behind. But then they began a dazzling, breakneck surge that saw them win 19 of 20 and pull within a game of the Dodgers.

At this point the Dodgers came to Busch Stadium for a three-game series, creating a World Series atmosphere in St. Louis. For those of long memory, the shootout carried a whiff of the old nostalgia: the Cardinals and the Dodgers (representing Los Angeles now, of course) playing a September set with the National League pennant tantalizingly afloat.

It was a memorable three-game series, with the memories ultimately tinted in Dodger blue rather than Cardinal red. Johnny Podres won the first game for L.A., 3–1, the estimable Sandy Koufax fired a 4–0 shutout in the second game, and the Dodgers made it a sweep with a 6–5, 13-inning victory in the finale. The Dodgers left town with a firm grip on first place that they never relinquished.

Ernie Broglio posted an 18–8 record for St. Louis (which soon turned out to be of great significance for St. Louis), Gibson was 18–9, and left-hander Curt Simmons, one-time ace fireballer of the Phillies whom Devine had reclaimed from the scrap heap, was 15–9, at the age of thirty-four winning with guile and slow curves.

White, Groat, and Flood each attained the

(OPPOSITE BOTTOM) August Busch (right) has just signed Stan Musial to the star's final contract in 1963. General manager Bing Devine is in the middle.

STANLEY FRANK MUSIAL
"THE MAN"

ST. LOUIS CARDINALS 1941-1963
HOLDS MANY NATIONAL LEAGUE RECORDS,
AMONG THEM: GAMES PLAYED 3026; AT
BAT 10972 TIMES; 3630 HITS; MOST RUNS
SCORED 1949; MOST RUNS BATTED IN 1951;
TOTAL BASES 6134. LED N.L. IN TOTAL
BASES 6 YEARS, SLUGGING PERCENTAGE
6 YEARS. MOST VALUABLE PLAYER 1943-
1946=1948. PLAYED IN 24 ALL-STAR GAMES.
LIFETIME BATTING AVERAGE .331.

(TOP) "It got a little tougher each year," Musial said. Here he is in the spring of 1963, getting into shape for his final season. (BOTTOM) Stan Musial's Hall of Fame plaque at Cooperstown.

165

Game-time action at old Busch Stadium (formerly Sportsman's Park) in the 1950s.

200-hit mark, with White and Boyer each driving in over 100 runs.

In addition to the tension and excitement of the September pennant run, there had been a sentimental dimension to the race, for Musial had announced that this would be his final season on the active rolls and Cardinal fans were hoping to see their all-time favorite go out a winner. But the forty-two-year-old Man and his teammates fell a few games short.

A .255 hitter in his 22nd and final year, Musial left the game as a prolific record holder. Those 22 years in St. Louis tied him with Mel Ott for the longest one-man, one-team tenure in National League history. Having broken Honus Wagner's National League record hit total several years before, Musial was setting a new standard with every safe rap. His 3,630th and last hit came on the final day of the season, after appropriate speeches and ceremonies to mark the occasion. The hit was a single, it came against the Cincinnati Reds, and as the ball winged its way toward the outfield grass it passed over the head of Cincinnati's twenty-two-year-old rookie second baseman Pete Rose, who two decades later would break Musial's record. Thus the continuity of baseball, the game of aging kings and restless crown princes.

PAY DIRT

AS THE TALE IS TOLD, THERE seem to have been two pennants in the National League in 1964—the one the Phillies didn't win and the one the Cardinals did. History has decided that the Phillies' end-of-the-season collapse is more noteworthy than the Cardinals' surge, leading Ken Boyer to mutter, "Hell, we won it just as much as they lost it."

The Cardinals ended with the same 93–69 record they had posted in 1963, but in 1964 it was good enough to give them a one-game pennant victory over Philadelphia and Cincinnati, who tied for second.

The race was this tight: Had the Cardinals lost their final game, they, the Phillies, and the Reds would have finished the season in a three-way deadlock. Also, it wasn't until the season's penultimate day that the fourth-place Giants were mathematically eliminated.

As late as July 24, Keane's club was freighted with a 47–48 record, ten games out of first place. Thereafter, they played at a torrid .687 pace—46–21, including a 21–8 September, the best month any National League team had all season. On August 24, they were in fourth place, 11 games behind. By September 2, however, they had trimmed the deficit to 6½.

On the morning of September 21, Gene Mauch's Phillies, with just 12 games left to play, held a 6½-game lead over second-place St. Louis and Cincinnati. At this point the Phillies suddenly dropped over a precipice—they lost ten games in a row. While the Phillies were plummeting, the Cardinals were winning eight straight and the Reds nine.

On September 27, the Reds moved into first place, one game ahead of the Phillies, 1½ over the Cardinals. The next day, the Phillies came to St. Louis for a three-game series and were swept, with Gibson, Sadecki, and Simmons doing the pitching. On October 1, the Cardinals were on top, a half game over the Reds and 2½ over the Phillies.

With a final three-game series scheduled against the hapless New York Mets—losers of 109 games that year—the Cardinals looked to be in good shape. On Friday, however, the Mets edged Gibson 1–0, while the Phillies finally ended their ten-game plunge by beating the Reds. The next day the Mets outdid them-

Barney Schultz (1955, 1963–65). His classy relief pitching helped the Cardinals to the pennant in 1964.

167

runs, and led the league with 119 RBIs, it was an MVP year.

The outfield was covered by Curt Flood (.311), Mike Shannon, Charlie James, and a newcomer who was about to burst into superstardom—Lou Brock.

The acquisition of Brock from the Cubs on June 15 was one of Bing Devine's finest moves as general manager (ironically, Devine was fired in August, just before the Cardinals drove themselves back into the race). Brock came to St. Louis with pitchers Paul Toth and Jack Spring, who quickly faded from the scene. To Chicago the Cardinals sent outfielder Doug Clemens, veteran left-hander Bobby Shantz, and Ernie Broglio. Broglio's 18 wins in 1963 had enchanted the Cubs and they had been determined to add the big right-hander. Ernie, however, never delivered for Chicago, winning

Curt Simmons (1960–66), who revived his career with the Cardinals after the Phillies had given up on him. He was an 18-game winner in 1964.

selves, tearing up Cardinal pitching in a 15–5 win. With the Reds idle, the Cardinals and Reds were now in a first-place tie. On the season's final day, the Cardinals' whipped the Mets 11–5 while the Phillies eliminated the Reds with a 10–0 pasting. St. Louis had won its tenth pennant and first in 18 years.

The Cardinals had many outstanding performances in 1964. The crack infield which as a unit had started the 1963 All-Star Game for the National League remained intact: White at first, Javier at second, Groat at short, and Boyer at third. For Boyer, who batted .295, hit 24 home

Right-hander Roger Craig (1964). He was 7–9 in his lone year in St. Louis. When the Cardinals defeated the San Francisco Giants in the 1987 playoffs, Craig was managing the Giants.

Curt Flood (1958–69). A stellar center fielder and six-time .300 hitter.

backstop Tim McCarver, at the age of twenty-two a shrewd catcher and sharp .288 hitter). Sadecki had the best of his 18 big-league seasons with a 20–11 record, Gibson was 19–12 with 245 strikeouts, and Simmons was 18–9. The club received its bullpen strength from Ron Taylor and thirty-eight-year-old knuckleballer Barney Schultz, called up from the minors on August 1. Barney got into thirty games, saving 14 and logging a 1.64 ERA.

It was the Cardinals' tenth World Series appearance, and for the fifth time their opponents were the New York Yankees, at the end now of an incredible dynasty that had seen the Bronx Bombers take fourteen pennants in sixteen years.

just seven games in three years before leaving the big leagues. As for Brock, not even the Cardinals realized how good he was.

Brock joined the Cardinals three days before his twenty-fifth birthday; he would remain until 1979. Lou had attended Southern University in Baton Rouge, majoring in mathematics. There the Cubs presented him with an irresistible number—$30,000—to sign a contract. In his first two years in Chicago, Brock batted .263 and .258 and was hitting .251 when the trade was made on June 15, 1964. For the remainder of the season, he batted .348 in 103 games for the Cardinals, ending the season with 43 stolen bases, second to the Dodgers' Maury Wills. Wills' revolutionary basepath exploits, begun with his record-breaking 104 steals in 1962, would be carried on and bettered by Brock. By the time he retired, Brock would have more than 3,000 hits, an all-time record 938 career stolen bases, and a place in the Hall of Fame.

The Cardinals had three strong starting pitchers in 1964 (who were mother-henned by

Lou Brock (1964–79): 938 lifetime stolen bases.

The infield of the 1964 National League pennant winners. *Left to right:* Ken Boyer, Dick Groat, Julian Javier, and Bill White.

(BOTTOM LEFT) Bill White. He batted over .300 and drove in more than 100 runs for three straight seasons (1962–64).

(BOTTOM RIGHT) A pair of left-handers who started the first game of the 1964 World Series. The Yankees' Whitey Ford *(left)* and the Cardinals' 20-game winner Ray Sadecki (1960–66, 1975).

Tim McCarver, who had 11 hits and a .478 batting average in the 1964 World Series.

The Yankees, managed by Yogi Berra, had a couple of prime-time gunners in Mickey Mantle and Roger Maris and some outstanding pitchers in Whitey Ford, Jim Bouton, Al Downing, and Mel Stottlemyre. The Cardinals, however, were about to turn Bob Gibson loose on World Series play.

The Series opened in St. Louis and the clubs split the first two games, Sadecki beating Ford, 9–5, and Stottlemyre beating Gibson, 8–3.

The three games at Yankee Stadium were tightly played crowd-pleasers. Game 3 went to the bottom of the ninth tied 1–1, thanks to

The classic follow-through of Bob Gibson.

THE St. LOUIS CARDINALS

the fine pitching of Simmons and Bouton. Schultz took over for St. Louis in the ninth, threw one pitch to Mantle, and the game was over. The Cardinals evened it up the next day, winning 4–3 on Boyer's grand slam in the top of the fifth (as he made his triumphal tour of the bases, Ken trotted past brother Clete, playing third for the Yankees). This game was won by the airtight relief pitching of Roger Craig and Ron Taylor, after Sadecki had been rocked by a three-run Yankee first. The Cardinals took Game 5 by a 5–2 score, the winning shot being McCarver's three-run homer in the top of the tenth. Gibson, striking out 13, was the winning pitcher.

Back in St. Louis, the Yankees forced a seventh game with an 8–3 win, Bouton beating Simmons, the Yankees blowing the game apart with a five-run eighth inning, culminating in Joe Pepitone's grand slammer.

Game 7 matched Gibson against Stottlemyre. Helped by home runs from Brock and Boyer, the Cardinals had a 6–0 lead after five. Some Yankee home run hitting tightened things up, but when it was over the Cardinals had won it, 7–5, Gibson going all the way and giving the Redbirds their seventh World Championship.

But the story wasn't over yet. Immediately after the Series, Yankee manager Yogi Berra was dismissed (the club claimed that Yogi had problems communicating with and controlling his players) and Johnny Keane resigned as Cardinal manager and was quickly signed to replace Berra.

Several explanations were offered for Keane's stunning departure in the wake of a World Series victory. Johnny had been unhappy with Devine's firing and had not developed a relationship with Bing's successor, Bob Howsam. Also, there had been rumors in August that Keane would be fired after the season (Leo Durocher was a rumored successor); but then the Cardinal surge to victory had saved the skipper's job. According to one story, Keane had resented the rumors, which he believed to be true, and decided to leave while enwreathed in victory. Another story, believed by those

whose ethics came hard-boiled, was that Keane had been tipped of Berra's imminent firing and that he would be offered the Yankee job, in those times an enviable and prestigious position.

In any event, Johnny went to New York and his timing couldn't have been worse—the Yankee dynasty was about to crumble as suddenly and completely as a dynamited building. The Yankees finished sixth in 1965 and after a 4–16 start in 1966, Keane was bounced. The tough little Irishman died of a heart attack less than a year later, only fifty-five years old.

Keane's replacement in St. Louis was not Leo Durocher but Red Schoendienst. The choice was a popular one. One of the most well-liked players in Cardinal history, Red had returned to the club in 1961 as utility second baseman and pinch-hitting specialist (he led the league with 22 pinch hits in 1962). His playing days were concluded in 1963 and he became a coach. And now, in 1965, he began a 12-year tenure as manager, longest in team history.

Schoendienst's first year as manager was a disappointing one as the world champs dropped to seventh place. Except for Gibson (20–12, 270 strikeouts) and Flood (.310), there was a general falling-off, though Brock began positioning himself as the heir to Maury Wills by stealing 63 bases, second to Maury's 94 (aside from Wills, Brock's stolen base total was the league's highest since 1912). The Redbird who experienced the sharpest decline was Sadecki, dropping from 20–11 in 1964 to 6–15 a year later.

Immediately after the 1965 season Howsam began giving the ball club a complete face lift. The first to go was Ken Boyer, dealt to the Mets·in exchange for third baseman Charley Smith and left-hander Al Jackson. A week later, Bill White, Dick Groat, and reserve catcher Bob Uecker went to the Phillies for catcher Pat Corrales, right-hander Art Mahaffey, and outfielder Alex Johnson. Uecker, like Joe Garagiola, was later to go on to become an announcer and TV personality. As a player, the chattery Uecker was known as a good defensive catcher, strong of arm, weak of bat, and, even then, irrepres-

Four smiling Redbirds obliging the cameraman. *Left to right:* Third baseman–outfielder Mike Shannon (1962–70), shortstop Dick Groat (1963–65), Julian Javier, and Tim McCarver.

sible of wit, which he was always willing to turn on himself. "Anybody with ability can play in the big leagues," he said. "But to be able to trick people year in and year out the way I did, I think that was a much greater feat." (Uecker spent six years in the bigs, playing with the Braves, Cardinals, and Phillies, batting an even .200 for 297 games.)

Neither of these trades noticeably helped the Cardinals, but the one Howsam engineered with the San Francisco Giants on May 8, 1966, did. In exchange for Ray Sadecki, the Cardinals obtained first baseman Orlando Cepeda. Cepeda had had some spectacular years for the Giants, but an ailing knee had all but washed

Catcher and future television personality Bob Uecker (1964–65). When he jokes about his hitting, he's not joking (.200 lifetime for six big-league seasons).

Lou Brock stealing base number 66 against Cincinnati in September 1966. Pete Rose is taking the throw.

out the 1965 season for him. The club had the knee examined, it was pronounced fit, and Cepeda became a Cardinal, going on to bat .301 in 1966, highest on the team.

Other outstanding Cardinal performances in 1966 included Brock's league-leading 74 stolen bases, Gibson's 21 victories and 225 strikeouts, and Curt Flood's 159 errorless games in center field (eight National League outfielders have fielded 1.000 in 100 games or more, but none played in as many games as Flood, who holds the league record with 226 consecutive errorless games and 568 consecutive chances, the latter the big-league mark).

The biggest St. Louis baseball news in 1966, however, was the opening of brand-new Busch Stadium on May 12, an event attended by a new one-game team record 46,048 paying customers.

With a seating capacity of more than 50,000, Busch Stadium was built south of the heart of the city's downtown area, on real estate located on the Mississippi River waterfront adjacent to Eero Saarinen's stainless steel Archway, a symbolic gateway rising some 630 feet into the air. Originally built with a natural grass playing surface, the field was converted to AstroTurf in

1970, a move that put a premium on speedy outfielders who could cut off drives hit into the gaps.

Symmetrical in its outfield dimensions, the stadium's foul lines are each 330 feet, the power alleys 386 feet, while straightaway center is 414. It is not an easy park for home runs and the Cardinals have consistently been among the league's lowest home run makers. Consequently, Cardinal teams have been designed, for the most part, to emphasize speed, defense, and pitching, qualities which have characterized many successful St. Louis Cardinal teams of the past.

The new Busch Stadium lured a team record 1,712,980 fans through the turnstiles, and they watched the team post a creditable 83–79 won-lost mark, which this year was only good enough for sixth place.

In 1967, however, playing their first full season in their new home, Schoendienst's club anointed it with another World Championship. In so doing, the team set another St. Louis attendance record, breaking the two million mark with 2,090,145 paid spectators, which would stand as the franchise's best until 1982.

The '67 Cardinals passed the 100-victory

mark for the fifth time in club history, posting a 101–60 record. What had been a tight race between the Cardinals and Cubs began to break apart at the end of July, when St. Louis began pulling away.

On July 25, the Cardinals and Cubs were tied with 56–40 records, with the two clubs engaging each other at Busch Stadium. The Cardinals won that night, won again the next day, and the seams of the pennant race began to tear apart. Schoendienst's men took 18 of their next 22 and by August 19 their lead was a solid 11½ games. Playing steady ball to the end, their final margin was 10½ games over second-place San Francisco.

For the tenth time since the award was instituted in 1931, the Cardinals had the league's Most Valuable Player, Orlando Cepeda, who put together a bruising year. The muscular first baseman, who was a unanimous choice for the award, hit 25 home runs and led the league with 111 RBIs. Tim McCarver, with a career-high .295 average, finished second in the balloting. Brock was again king of the base-stealers with 52, and Flood batted a personal-high .335.

In right field, the club had a most famous name—Roger Maris. The all-time single-season home run record holder had been obtained from the Yankees in a swap for Charley Smith. It was six years since Roger poled his "61 in '61" and a hand injury had robbed him of the might of his home run swing. Going with the pitch more and more, Maris batted .261 and hit just nine home runs.

On the mound, the Cardinals were long on talent and short on experience as Gibson was surrounded by an array of relative newcomers. The St. Louis pitching depth proved to be cru-

Busch Stadium, St. Louis, which opened for business on May 12, 1966.

Skipper Red Schoendienst with 1967's National League MVP Orlando Cepeda (1966–68).

Orlando Cepeda (*left*) and Roger Maris (1967–68), who retired after the '68 season at the age of thirty-four.

Arm miseries finished Dick Hughes' career after a fine 16–6 season in 1967. He pitched for St. Louis from 1966 to 1968.

cial. On July 13, in the midst of another strong season, Gibson suffered a broken leg when he was struck by a Roberto Clemente line drive (the gritty right-hander tried to stay in the game, even pitched to another batter, before being taken out). It was assumed he would be lost for the season, but Gibson was back in six weeks, ending with a 13–7 record.

The void created by Gibson's loss was filled by right-handers Dick Hughes, Ray Washburn, Nelson Briles, and left-hander Steve Carlton. Hughes was a twenty-nine-year-old rookie who surprised everyone with a 16–6 record (it proved to be a one-year stroll in the sunshine; his career was soon wiped out by a sore arm). Briles was 14–5 and Washburn 10–7. The twenty-two-year-old Carlton, in his first full year, was 14–9. Righty Ron Willis and lefty Joe Hoerner buoyed the bullpen.

Awaiting the Cardinals in the World Series was one of baseball's all-time Cinderella teams, the Boston Red Sox, who had made "The Impossible Dream" a delightful reality for all of New England. A ninth-place club the year before, the Sox had risen and followed the magic bat of Triple Crown–winner Carl Yastrzemski and the golden arm of right-hander Jim Lonborg and on the last day of the season won what had been an exhausting four-team pennant race.

But the romantic reverie of The Impossible Dream received a jarring awakening in the World Series, though not before a full, hard-played seven games. For the Cardinals, who usually gave baseball America its money's worth in October, it was their sixth full-term Series.

With Lonborg having worked in Boston's pennant clincher on the season's final day, the Red Sox opened with right-hander Jose Santiago. The Cardinals had Gibson primed for the Fenway Park curtain raiser. Santiago pitched

(TOP) Right-hander Nelson Briles (1965–70). He was a 19-game winner in 1968. (BOTTOM) Right-hander Ray Washburn (1961–69). His best was 14–8 in 1968.

Steve Carlton (1965–71), like Mordecai Brown, another great pitcher the Cardinals let get away.

well and even hit a home run for Boston's only run, but Gibson was on the way to all-time World Series stardom. The Cardinal ace fanned ten and whipped the Sox 2–1, abetted by Brock (also about to be covered in October stardust), who had four singles in four at bats, two stolen bases, and two runs scored, driven in each time by a Maris ground ball.

Game 2 belonged to Lonborg, who stopped the Cardinals 5–0 on one hit—a two-out double by Javier in the eighth. With two home runs and four RBIs, Yastrzemski joined Lonborg in the hero's circle. Hughes was the losing pitcher.

Game 3, in St. Louis, saw Briles stop the Sox, 5–2. Brock, the man to watch in this Series, singled and tripled and scored twice. The Cardinals took a formidable three games to one advantage with a 6–0 Gibson shutout in Game 4. Brock had a single and double, scored once, and stole a base. Boston stayed alive with a 3–1 Game 5 win, Lonborg pitching a three-hitter in beating Carlton.

Schoendienst used a Series-record eight pitchers in a losing cause in Game 6, four of them in the bottom of the eighth when Boston scored four times to break a 4–4 tie and go on to an 8–4 win. Hughes had started but reliever Jack Lamabe took the loss. Boston set a Series record when Yastrzemski, Reggie Smith, and Rico Petrocelli all hit home runs in the bottom of the fourth against Hughes. For St. Louis, Brock had two singles, three RBIs, scored twice, and stole a base.

With the Series now deadlocked, it looked like Boston might weave one last miracle and come back from a 3–1 deficit in games. It would be ace against ace—Gibson versus Lonborg (who had yielded just four hits in 18

Bob Gibson, the all-time Cardinal team leader in wins (251), complete games (255), innings (3,885), strikeouts (3,117), and shutouts (56).

That's Lou Brock stealing second in the first inning of Game 1 of the 1967 World Series. Boston's Rico Petrocelli is awaiting the throw. Frank Umont is the umpire.

innings). The St. Louis ace had one crucial edge—he would be working on three days' rest as opposed to two for Lonborg.

Lonborg began running out of gas early. The Cardinals scored two in the top of the third, two more in the fifth, and then a crushing three more in the sixth on Javier's three-run homer. Gibson was strong throughout, pitching a three-hitter, fanning ten, and, probably tastiest of all to him, hitting a home run in the fifth inning. It was a 7–2 World Championship victory for St. Louis. Brock crowned an already superbly productive Series with a single, double, and three stolen bases, giving him a Series record of seven thefts.

Julian Javier, second baseman on three Cardinal pennant winners.

179

Lou Brock, ready to travel.

For Gibson, it was an overpowering 3–0 World Series (and five straight October victories, going back to 1964), with 26 strikeouts in 27 innings and a 1.00 ERA. Brock had 12 hits and a .414 batting average, and Maris had ten hits, seven RBIs, and a .385 average.

For Stan Musial it had been a brief, highly successful run as Cardinal general manager. The Man had taken the job after Howsam left to go to Cincinnati, but now the pressures of outside business were putting too heavy a burden on Musial's time and he was forced to relinquish his front-office portfolio. Musial's replacement was a familiar face—Bing Devine, who had been working in New York as president of the Mets.

The Cardinals took consecutive pennants for the third time in their history in 1968, a season remembered in baseball annals as "The Year of the Pitcher." And the pitcher of the year in the National League was Bob Gibson, who scorched his way through one of the most con-

sistently dominating summers ever delivered from any mound.

Gibson in 1968 created a landmark season, a season of such impressive dimensions that it remains like fire in the baseball skies. His won-lost record was 22–9, standard enough for an ace, though at one point in the season he was 3–5; it was his ERA of 1.12 that made his year memorable. That figure, which is to the pitching fraternity what Ted Williams' .406 batting average in 1941 is to the hitters', established a major league standard for a pitcher with 300 or more innings (he pitched 305).

Along with that parsimonious ERA, Gibson led the league with 268 strikeouts and 13 shutouts (only Grover Cleveland Alexander, with 16 blankers in dead-ball 1916, ever had more in a big-league season). In the month of June, Gibson delivered five shutouts, had a run of 48 straight scoreless innings and then 95 innings during which he gave up just two runs. At one point he had 15 consecutive wins, ten of them

An unhappy Dick Hughes gazes down at the mound as Boston's Rico Petrocelli circles the bases after homering in the second inning of Game 6 of the 1967 Series.

Bob Gibson (right) about to shake hands with Tim McCarver after defeating the Red Sox in the seventh game of the 1967 World Series.

The two right-handers who were dominant in 1968, "The Year of the Pitcher," and who started the opening game of that year's World Series: Detroit's Denny McLain (left) and Bob Gibson.

National League President Warren Giles (left) making a double presentation to Bob Gibson. Giles is holding Gibson's Cy Young Award, while Bob is holding his Most Valuable Player Award, both earned for his super performance in 1968.

shutouts. He completed 28 of 34 starts and was never once driven from the mound in the middle of an inning. He was the National League MVP and was unanimously the Cy Young Award winner.

It was one of the team's easier pennants. By the end of July they held a 6½-game lead; by August 1 they were 15 ahead, with their final margin nine games over the Giants.

The Cardinals batted just .248, but in The Year of the Pitcher that was better than six other teams in the ten-team league. Curt Flood's .301 led the Redbirds. Orlando Cepeda dropped sharply from his MVP season, hitting 16 home runs (most on the team, which hit only 73) and batting .248. Brock's 62 stolen bases gave him the lead for the third straight year.

Led by Gibson, the staff's 2.49 ERA was the best in the league. Briles was 19–11, Washburn 14–8, and Carlton 13–11. Symbolizing the year's feathery hitting were two games between the Cardinals and Giants on September 17–18. On the 17th, the Giants' Gaylord Perry no-hit Schoendienst's men, 1–0. The next day, Washburn turned it around with precision, firing the Cardinals' first no-hitter since War-

Kaline to tie the record. A few moments later he struck out Norm Cash to break the record, and a few moments after that he ended the game in blazing style by striking out Willie Horton, making it 17 whiffs, two better than the old mark. Adding luster to the flourish was the fact that Kaline, Cash, and Horton were Detroit's three best hitters.

In Game 2, left-hander Mickey Lolich and the Tigers evened it up with an 8–2 belting of Briles. Game 3, in Detroit, was a 7–3 Cardinal victory, Washburn winning, with three-and-two-thirds scoreless relief innings from lefty Joe Hoerner, the club's bullpen ace this year. McCarver and Cepeda each contributed three-run homers and Brock had three singles and three stolen bases.

Outfielder Bobby Tolan (1965–68), who had several years of stardom after being traded to the Reds in 1969.

Lou Brock. His 2,713 hits in a Cardinal uniform rank second in team history to Stan Musial's 3,630.

neke's in 1941, stopping the Giants by a score of 2–0.

The American League pennant winners were the Detroit Tigers, and this created a match-up between the two ace right-handers who excelled during The Year of the Pitcher—Gibson and Detroit's 31-game winner Dennis McLain, baseball's first thirty-game winner since Dizzy Dean in 1934 (a year that also featured a Cardinal-Tiger Series).

The Series opened in St. Louis and the avidly anticipated duel of aces saw Gibson emerge the winner, 4–0, helped by a home run by Brock, who for the second year in a row was going to put on a sizzling October display of his many talents. The game turned out to be a Gibson spectacular. By the bottom of the ninth the St. Louis speedballer had notched 14 strikeouts, one below the Series record set by Sandy Koufax in 1963.

Mickey Stanley opened Detroit's ninth inning with a single. Gibson then fanned Al

Nelson Briles firing the first pitch of Game 2 of the 1968 Series. The batter is Detroit's Dick McAuliffe. Tim McCarver is the catcher, Jim Honochick the umpire.

Game 4 brought Gibson and McLain back to the mound, and again it was Gibson, winning his record seventh straight World Series game (all complete efforts), 10–1, as the Cardinals disposed of McLain early. Gibson fanned ten and helped his cause with a home run. For Brock it was another three-hit game—single, double, home run, stolen base, and four RBIs.

The Cardinals were now poised to win another World Championship. But Lolich, despite giving up three runs in the top of the first inning, held them off in Game 5, defeating Briles, 5–3. For the third game in a row Brock collected three hits.

The Series returned to St. Louis, the Cardinals still needing just one victory for a wrap. But Game 6 blew up in their faces in the top of the third when the Tigers demolished Washburn and several relievers in a ten-run inning. With McLain turning in his best outing of the Series, the Tigers won easily, 13–1, leaving it up to a seventh game.

With the invincible Gibson facing Lolich (working on two days' rest), the Cardinals felt sanguine about their chances. For six innings it was a seventh World Series game as a seventh

World Series game should be—scoreless. But in the top of the seventh inning the Tigers broke through, with a bit of help from a most unlikely source. With men on first and second and two out, Jim Northrup lifted a fly to deep center. As he broke back on the ball, Flood stumbled, and the otherwise catchable ball sailed on and struck the ground and rolled on for a triple. Northrup scored a moment later and it was 3–0. The final count was 4–1, the Cardinals scoring on Mike Shannon's two-out, ninth-inning homer.

The Cardinals had played a full-length World Series for the seventh time; they had won the previous six, but this time the winds had changed, for both the team and for Bob Gibson, whose seven-game World Series winning streak had come to an end. As fiercely competitive and bluntly outspoken as he was, Gibson was too much the professional to blame Flood for the heartbreaking loss.

"That man has won or saved many a ballgame for me," Gibson said of his center fielder.

For Brock it had been a second straight brilliant October outing. The Cardinal flash batted .464, tied a Series record with 13 hits, and tied his own record by again stealing seven bases.

DOWN FROM
THE MOUNTAIN

THE CARDINALS HAD DEMON-strated a knack for winning pennants by the handful—five between 1926 and 1934, four between 1942 and 1946, and now three between 1964 and 1968. But it would be fourteen years before they returned to the winner's circle, having to be satisfied with a couple of near-misses as the 1970s turned out to be as dry a decade for them as the 1950s had been.

Expansion came to the National League in 1969 (San Diego and Montreal joining the lodge) and with it divisional play was introduced. With someone in the league office evidently having flunked geography, St. Louis wound up in the East Division (with Atlanta being designated a Western club).

Schoendienst's men finished fourth in their six-team division in 1969, winning a substantial 87 games. Nine teams, in fact, won over 80 games this year, thanks to the bedraggled records of San Diego and Montreal (52–110 each) and Philadelphia (63–99).

The most significant addition to the Cardinals was Joe Torre, obtained from Atlanta for Orlando Cepeda in a swap of first basemen. Joe batted .289 and drove in 101 runs. Brock was at .298 and his 53 stolen bases gave him the lead for the fourth straight time.

Gibson was 20–13 with 269 strikeouts, 2.18 ERA, and a league-high 28 complete games. Advancing steadily toward stardom, Steve Carlton was 17–11, with 210 whiffs and 2.17 ERA. Carlton pitched the game of the year at Busch Stadium on the night of September 15,

and by his very brilliance demonstrated the futility of trying to beat a team that for a single year had been anointed. Working against "The Miracle Mets," who that year rose from a ninth-place finish in 1968 to become history's most improbable world champions, Carlton set a new one-game major league record by nailing 19 Mets on strikes. Unfortunately, he also fed

Steve Carlton.

Right-hander Mike Torrez (1967–71), who began his long major league career with St. Louis. He was 10–4 in 1969.

a couple of two-run homers to Ron Swoboda, in the fourth and eighth innings, enough for a 4–3 Mets victory.

After the season, on October 7, Devine made a seven-player trade with the Phillies that lit fires of controversy that eventually burned all the way to the United States Supreme Court.

The Cardinals sent to the Phillies Curt Flood, Tim McCarver, Joe Hoerner, and outfielder Byron Browne, in exchange for first baseman Richie (later "Dick") Allen, second baseman Cookie Rojas, and pitcher Jerry Johnson. Allen was a highly talented power hitter with a reputation for roiling the waters; it was, however, the reserved and gentlemanly Flood who created the controversy.

The idea of being traded offended Flood; he felt it was an affront to his dignity as a human being. The Phillies tried to mollify him with a $100,000 contract—generous for the time—but Flood was standing on principle. He sued to become a free agent, asserting that the "reserve clause" in his contract—making him the lifetime "property" of whatever club held his contract—constituted involuntary servitude and was therefore unconstitutional. The Supreme Court, however, upheld the status quo, although conceding that the reserve clause was an "anomaly" in that day and age that Congress might well examine.

Flood never reported to Philadelphia, choosing to sit out the 1970 season while his case was being argued. He joined the Washington Senators in 1971, played in a handful of games, and then retired. He was thirty-three years old.

To compensate the Phillies for Flood, the Cardinals sent them a pair of minor leaguers, one of whom was outfielder–first baseman Willie Montanez, who went on to have a long and productive career, playing for nine different teams.

The talented and troublesome Richie Allen (1970).

Ted Sizemore firing it to first to complete the double play as the Cubs' Jose Cardenal slides in. Sizemore played second base for the Cardinals from 1971 to 1975.

was and as personally likable, there was always an employer eager to help him pack his bags and drive him to the airport.

The Cardinals felt comfortable about trading McCarver because they were ready to break in behind the plate Ted Simmons, a twenty-year-old switch-hitter who would soon rank among baseball's top catchers.

The team finished fourth in 1970, despite the hitting of Allen and some solid whacking from Torre (21 homers, 100 RBIs, .325 batting average) and Brock (202 hits, .304 average). Gibson's 23–7 record and 274 strikeouts earned him his second Cy Young Award. Carlton, however, dropped to 10–19, leading the league in losses, thus joining a curious circle—great or near-great pitchers who led the league in defeats, their numbers including Phil Niekro, Paul Derringer, and Hall of Famers Red Ruffing and Robin Roberts, among others.

In 1971, the Cardinals bobbed around the fringes of the pennant race. They were in and

In Allen, the Cardinals were getting one of the league's premier boppers and one of its larger headaches. No one questioned Richie's talent (which included, in Casey Stengel's words, "hitting them over buildings"), nor could anyone quibble about the effort he put out on the field. It was getting him to the field and getting him there on time that led to the graying of various managers. Allen followed his own tides and currents, which sometimes brought him to occasions like spring training, batting practice, and game time a bit later than the rest of his immediate fraternity. An occasional missed plane might drop him a full day behind things.

Allen played just one season in St. Louis and did well—34 home runs and 101 RBIs in 122 games. Immediately after the season, however, he was traded to the Dodgers for second baseman Ted Sizemore. Allen played for four different teams in four years. As talented as he

Ted Simmons (1968–80). He batted over .300 six times, with a high of .332 in 1975.

Infield handyman Phil Gagliano (1963–70).

out. It was Bullet Bob's 201st career win and its magnitude surprised him.

"I never expected to get one," Gibson said, "because I'm a high-ball pitcher and high-ball pitchers don't pitch no-hitters."

The supremely self-confident, moodily impassive right-hander surprised himself in another way: He admitted that at the end he was nervous, saying that he "couldn't believe it. I never got nervous before, not even in the World Series."

For Joe Torre, it was a spectacular season. Playing third base now, he won the batting

out of first place through April and May, but then a 9–22 June tied an anchor to their dreams that hung to them for the rest of the summer. They got within four games of first-place Pittsburgh on August 15, but never closer, settling for a second-slot windup, seven games out.

Gibson, who dropped to 16–13, fired his only big-league no-hitter against the Pirates on August 14, fanning Willie Stargell for the final

Bob Gibson in the Busch Stadium clubhouse.

Joe Torre (1969–74). He was the batting champ and league MVP in 1971.

stantial increase, to a salary rumored to be around $75,000, which was more than the club wanted to pay. The difference of opinion finally became a confrontation between two strong-willed men—Steve Carlton and August Busch—and it was resolved with Carlton being traded to Philadelphia for right-hander Rick Wise, a good pitcher but not of world-class stature, which Carlton was about to become as he turned in a spectacular 27–10 record (for a club that won just 59 games), 1.97 ERA, and 310 strikeouts, winning the first of his four Cy Young Awards.

Schoendienst's club could do no better than fourth in 1972, 21½ games behind. For the thirty-six-year-old Gibson, it was a final season of high production—19–11, 208 strikeouts. Wise was 16–16 and right-hander Reggie Cleveland 14–15. With 63 stolen bases, Brock was the leader for the sixth time.

The caprices of divisional play were never more evident than in the National League East

title with a .363 average, led in hits with 230 and RBIs with 137, hit 24 home runs, and became the eleventh Cardinal to win the MVP Award.

Brock, who had lost the stolen base crown to Bobby Tolan the year before, reclaimed it in 1971 with 64 successful swipes. Lou's .313 average, young Simmons' .304, and outfielder Matty Alou's .315 gave the club four .300 hitters and a league-high .275 average. (Alou had come to St. Louis in a deal that saw Nelson Briles go to Pittsburgh.)

For Carlton, 10–19 in 1970, it was a brilliant turnaround year, the big left-hander ringing up a 20–9 record, a record that, ironically, led to his being traded to the Phillies in one of the most unfortunate transactions in Cardinal history.

After his big season, Carlton asked for a sub-

Matty Alou (1971–73), a .315 hitter in 1971.

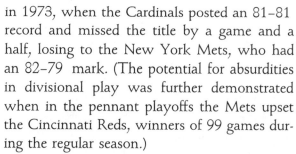

Left-hander Jerry Reuss (1969–71). He was 14–14 in 1971. Like Carlton, he was destined to do his best pitching for another team.

Rick Wise (1972–73), a 16-game winner in each of his years with St. Louis.

in 1973, when the Cardinals posted an 81–81 record and missed the title by a game and a half, losing to the New York Mets, who had an 82–79 mark. (The potential for absurdities in divisional play was further demonstrated when in the pennant playoffs the Mets upset the Cincinnati Reds, winners of 99 games during the regular season.)

It would have been a ragged championship, but the Cardinals would have taken it, and almost did. Early August saw them holding a five-game lead, which was remarkable considering they had lost 12 of their first 13 games and 20 of their first 25. But then they spun into an eight-game wining streak. A seven-game losing streak in September dealt them a blow from which they never recovered.

The Cardinals played the last two months under a severe handicap—the loss of Bob Gibson, who tore ligaments in his leg while sliding into a base in a game in New York on August 4 and pitched only once more for the rest of the season. Without Gibson, the staff seemed to go adrift. Wise did not win a game between

August 5 and September 21, though finishing with a 16–12 record, while Cleveland (14–10) won just one game after August 22. Gibson was 12–10.

Simmons batted .310 (his third straight year over .300) while catching 153 games, and Brock (.297) again led in stolen bases with 70. Now thirty-four years old, Brock was doing something quite unusual—the older he was getting the more bases he was stealing. Simmons and Torre led the team in home runs with 13 apiece, lowest for a Redbird team leader since 1943.

Devine was busy in postseason wheeling and dealing, particularly with the Boston Red Sox. On October 26, 1973, the GM sent Wise and outfielder Bernie Carbo to Boston for outfielder Reggie Smith and pitcher Ken Tatum. Later, on December 7, pitchers Reggie Cleveland, Diego Segui, and infielder Terry Hughes were dispatched to Boston for a trio of pitchers: Lynn McGlothen, Mike Garman, and lefty John Curtis.

A year later, with all the roster additions and

Right-hander Reggie Cleveland (1969–73).

subtractions, the arithmetic came out exactly the same—second place, 1½ games behind, this time trailing Pittsburgh. The Cardinals could look back wistfully on a July swoon of 13 losses in 14 games, a dip that took them from three ahead to three behind. Still, they remained in the race, thanks to an 18–9 September.

Bernie Carbo (1972–73, 1979–80) scoring as the ball gets away from Pittsburgh catcher Manny Sanguillen. The action occurred in September 1973. Carbo was traded to Boston after the 1973 season.

The night of September 25 saw a truly memorable contest at Busch Stadium, the Cardinals versus the Pirates, who at game time led Schoendienst's club by a half game. The Pirates broke a 9–9 tie with three runs in the top of the 11th, only to have the Cardinals come roaring back with four, to take a thrilling 13–12 victory and a half-game lead in first place. After that, however, the Cardinals took three of their last five while the Pirates were winning six of seven and the division.

The Cardinals' September excitement included a marathon against the Mets on September 11 at New York's Shea Stadium, a 25-inning affair that the Cardinals finally won, 4–3. It was the longest night game by innings in major league history, the longest game in Cardinal history, and second longest (by one inning) in major league annals.

With Gibson continuing to decline—he was

Dal Maxvill (1962–72), light of stick, but a superb shortstop, and a future general manager.

Right-hander Lynn McGlothen (1974–76), who won 16 games in 1974.

11–13 in 1974—the ace of the staff was McGlothen, who logged a 16–12 mark. The top reliever was Al Hrabosky, a colorful, crowd-pleasing left-hander who at times sported a Fu Manchu facial decoration that made him look fierce, and who threw a fastball that came in with a rush. The self-styled "Mad Hungarian"—part of whose performance was turning his back on the batter, walking toward second base, stopping, "meditating," then whirling around and returning to the mound—was 8–1, with nine saves.

St. Louis had an all-.300-hitting outfield that year: Reggie Smith .309, Brock .306, and Rookie of the Year Bake McBride .309. Although dipping to .272, Simmons drove in 103 runs, giving the club two switch-hitters (Smith being the other) with 100 or more RBIs.

Aside from the pulsing pennant race, the biggest story in St. Louis baseball in 1974 was Brock, who this year broke Maury Wills's one-year stolen base record. Generally, when one-year records are broken it is by a slim margin; it is almost mandatory that they be. Brock, however, set his new mark like a titan—118 steals to Wills's 1962 standard of 104.

The record was broken at Busch Stadium on the night of September 10, against the Phillies, when, with a large crowd egging him on with "Go, go, go," Brock, who had 29 swipes in August, stole bases number 104 and 105.

Adding to the stature of Brock's achievement was the fact that he was setting a stolen base record at the age of thirty-five, which, as someone remarked, "is like a ten-year-old horse winning the Kentucky Derby." Brock was caught in the act 33 times. When Rickey Hen-

Relief ace Al ("The Mad Hungarian") Hrabosky (1970–77).

Reggie Smith (1974–76), the talented, switch-hitting outfielder, who twice batted over .300 for the Cardinals.

derson broke Brock's record in 1982 (at the age of twenty-four) with 130 steals, he was caught 42 times.

The near-misses of 1973–74 proved to be high-water marks for the Cardinals in the 1970s. The club finished third in '75, a year that marked a transition of sorts. It was a farewell swing through the schedule for Bob Gibson, who at the age of thirty-nine was reduced to a 3–10 season. Gibson left the big leagues with a 251–174 career mark, 3,117 strikeouts,

Bake McBride (1973–77), National League Rookie of the Year in 1974. A steady .300 hitter, Bake reached a high of .335 in 1976.

and 56 shutouts, leaving behind Cardinal records for wins, strikeouts, shutouts, and complete games (255).

With Torre having been traded to the Mets (for Ray Sadecki, whom the Cardinals had once traded for Orlando Cepeda, who was traded for Torre in the first place), Smith played first base until the club installed at the position twenty-one-year-old Keith Hernandez, a handsome line-drive hitter soon to make the Gold Glove his own personal award.

The '75 club topped the league with a .273 batting average, led by Simmons's career-high .332. Ted caught 154 games and drove in 100 runs, but the talented Cardinal was doomed to be overshadowed at the position by Cincin-

How hot is a St. Louis summer? Well, hot enough for Lou Brock to strap an umbrella to his head during batting practice.

Outfielder Jose Cruz (1970–74), who was traded to Houston, where he had a fine career.

for twenty-year-old switch-hitting shortstop Garry Templeton, who got into 53 games and batted .291. The cast was further changed in June when Reggie Smith was traded to the Dodgers for three players who did little to help the Cardinals.

With a 72–90 record, the Redbirds had lost more games than any Cardinal team since 1916, and this finally punched the ticket for Red Schoendienst. After twelve years, the longest reign of any Cardinal manager, the popular old second baseman was let go after the 1976 season (he returned in 1979 as a coach, a position he was to hold for many years).

Hoping to instill a more aggressive attitude in the club, Devine chose to replace the soft-spoken Schoendienst with the tough-talking disciplinarian Vern Rapp, formerly a catcher in

Ted Simmons.

nati's Johnny Bench. Smith batted .302, McBride .300, and Brock, with 56 stolen bases, .309. After 11 straight years with over 180 hits per season, the great St. Louis thoroughbred had just 163 safe raps, the first indication of the coming twilight.

Right-hander Bob Forsch, who would have one of the longest careers of any Cardinal pitcher, was 15–10, while Hrabosky burned up the late innings with a 13–3 record, 1.67 ERA, and league-high 22 saves.

The club dropped to fifth place in 1976, despite another .300-hitting outfield—Brock .301, McBride .335, and Willie Crawford .304. Crawford, who had been acquired from the Dodgers for Ted Sizemore, played just the one year for the Cardinals. Right-hander John Denny was the ERA leader (2.52) despite a so-so 11–9 record.

Brock stole 56 bases, going over 50 swipes for the 12th time and 12th consecutive time, both big-league records. It was a break-in year

Rookie Keith Hernandez in 1975. He was an excellent hitter and superlative first baseman for the
Cards from 1974 to 1983.

Right-hander John Denny (1974–79), the National
League's ERA leader in 1976. He would later win a
Cy Young Award with Philadelphia.

Right-hander Bob Forsch (1974–88). The longtime Redbird had his top year in 1977 when he was 20–7.

(ABOVE TOP AND BOTTOM) Lou Brock roaring in for his record-making 893rd career stolen base. It occurred in San Diego on August 29, 1977. Shortstop Bill Almon is covering.

the St. Louis organization and more recently a manager in the American Association. Rapp ran the club through a moderately successful season, 83 victories and a third-place finish. Templeton was now the regular shortstop and in his first full year batted .322, had 200 hits, and led the league with 18 triples. Bob Forsch was 20–7, the best year of his long career.

Since the beginning of the season it had been obvious that sometime during the summer Lou Brock was going to break Ty Cobb's lifetime record of 892 stolen bases. The St. Louis 90-foot-dash expert had ended the 1976 season with 865 thefts, just 27 short of Cobb's mark.

On August 29, 1977, at San Diego, Brock

(OPPOSITE BOTTOM) Lou Brock racking up another stolen base, this one against the New York Mets. Shortstop Frank Taveras (left) and second baseman Doug Flynn never had a chance.

finally completed the climb he had begun with the Cubs fifteen years before, and passed this particular Cobb marker with career steals number 892 and 893, shattering yet another "unbreakable" record (just a few years before, Hank Aaron had broken Ruth's long-standing lifetime total of 714 home runs). It was a crowning moment for the thirty-eight-year-old star, whose .272 batting average this season was his lowest since 1963.

As a manager, Vern Rapp frequently took a distinctly old-fashioned approach to his job and, as applied to the free-spirited player of the

197

The Phillies' Ted Sizemore is trying to shove Garry Templeton to break up a double play in this September 1977 action. Garry still got his man.

Shortstop Garry Templeton (1976–81). A .300 hitter, he led the league in triples for three straight years (1977–79).

Ted Simmons defending home plate against Pittsburgh's Dave Parker in action from April 1978.

1970s, this was a clear liability. The skipper's strict approach to team discipline and his occasional intemperate remarks about a player's abilities had opened a gap between manager and team, and the gap was not getting narrower. In his excellent history of the Cardinals, *Redbirds*, longtime St. Louis sportswriter Bob Broeg suggests that a thoughtless reference to Ted Simmons as a "loser" might have turned the thinning ice under Rapp into pure water. In any event, fifteen games into the 1978 season, with the club record standing at the Woolworth figure—5 and 10—Vern Rapp was dismissed.

Replacing Rapp was a man of purest Redbird pedigree, Ken Boyer, who had closed out his playing career in 1969 and then gone on to manage in the minor leagues for seven years.

The club that Boyer inherited was not hitting like Cardinal units of old, their .249 team average in 1978 being ninth in the 12-team league. Templeton, though again leading in triples (13), dropped 42 points to .280, Hernandez slumped to .255, and Brock to .221. If not for the fact that he closed the season with 2,900 hits and dearly wanted to reach 3,000, Lou would no doubt have retired. But Boyer believed his former teammate had one good year left and Ken was supported by August Busch, something of a sentimentalist when it came to his great stars.

The club was in last place much of the sum-

mer, finally climbed out in August, and finished fifth. Denny topped the staff with a 14–11 record, while the pitching highlight of the season came early, when Bob Forsch no-hit the Phillies on April 16, 5–0. (A year later his brother Ken pitched a similar gem for Houston, making them the first brothers ever to pitch no-hitters.)

Bing Devine left the Cardinal front office for the second time after the 1978 season, replaced by John Claiborne, who left the Boston Red Sox to come to St. Louis.

Claiborne, whose stay in St. Louis would be relatively brief, saw some hefty hitting lift the club to third place in 1979—the Cardinals led the league with a .278 average, highest for a Redbird outfit since 1954. Leading the team as

Pete Vuckovich (1978–80). The rugged righty won 15 games in 1979.

Switch-hitting outfielder Jerry Mumphrey (1974–79). His best was .295 in 1979.

200

Third baseman Ken Reitz (1972–75, 1977–80), who was a fine defensive player.

ticing and treasured number 3,000, which came on the night of August 13, when Lou rapped a sharp single off of Cubs right-hander Dennis Lamp. At the close of the season Brock rode off into the sunset to await his beckoning from Cooperstown (it came in 1985), leaving with an all-time-high 938 career stolen bases.

Brock's retirement helped close out the decade for the Cardinals as well as an era in club history. He had joined the team in 1964, a year after the retirement of Musial, won pennants with Ken Boyer, Bill White, Bob Gibson, Curt Flood, Orlando Cepeda, Tim McCarver, and other St. Louis highlight names.

The club would resurrect in the 1980s, following an "every other decade" pattern of success: four pennants in the 1940s, three in the 1960s, and now another decade of success ahead. The chief architect of this revival was one of the game's most vivid characters, a well-

well as the league was Hernandez, who jumped his average 89 points to .344. The magic-gloved first baseman stacked up 210 hits, 105 RBIs, and led the league in doubles (48) and runs (116). This sparkling season earned him the Most Valuable Player Award, which he shared with Pittsburgh's Willie Stargell in the first ever tie vote for an MVP designation.

Hernandez was the top gun in a lineup that smoked with five .300 hitters: Templeton .314, Brock .304, second baseman Ken Oberkfell .301, and outfielder George Hendrick .300. Templeton's 19 triples gave him the lead for the third straight year, tying the major league record.

For Brock it was a triumphant final season, as he came back from a .221 year in 1978 to surprise and delight the Cardinals with a .304 batting average and 123 hits, including that en-

Mike Tyson (1972–79), who gave the Cardinals some good service at second and at short.

Lou Brock celebrating hit number 3,000 on August 13, 1979.

traveled, case-hardened baseball lifer—Whitey Herzog. He would be freewheeling and aggressive, and he would shape the Cardinals into one of the most exciting and successful teams of the 1980s.

It looks like there's a knotty problem for Whitey Herzog.

WHITEY AND THE EIGHTIES

DORREL ("WHITEY") HERZOG was a baseball-happy kid who was born in 1931 in New Athens, Illinois, a farming and coal-mining town about thirty miles southeast of St. Louis, to where he would catch rides as a youngster and go and watch the Cardinals play.

Originally signed by the Yankees, Whitey reached the majors with the Washington Senators in 1956 as a left-handed-hitting outfielder. He subsequently played with Kansas City, Baltimore, and Detroit, leaving the active rolls in 1963 with a career average of .257.

Whitey's second career started as a scout for the Kansas City A's in 1964, after which he coached for KC and then in 1966 the New York Mets. From 1967 through 1972 he worked as the Mets' Director of Player Development, leaving that job in 1973 to manage the Texas Rangers, remaining in that thankless post only until early September.

After working as a coach for the California Angels, in July 1975 Whitey took over as manager of the Kansas City Royals and began a run of great success. In four full seasons with the Royals, he won three division titles and in his fourth year finished second. Each of his division winners, however, failed to make it successfully through the pennant playoffs, and this created a growing frustration within the inner chambers of the KC hierarchy, and when Whitey finished second in 1979 they pulled the plug on him.

In early June 1980, the Cardinals were stumbling badly—they were in the midst of an 18–33 record—and the front office decided to make a managerial change: Ken Boyer was out and Whitey Herzog was in.

Herzog took over a good-hitting but weak-pitching club. The 1980 Cardinals, who finished fourth, again led the league in batting (.275) as well as five other offensive categories. The lineup was stocked with six .300 hitters in Hernandez (who batted .321, losing the batting title by three points to Chicago's Bill Buckner), Oberkfell, Templeton, Hendrick, Simmons, and part-timer Dane Iorg.

It was a year of changes for the Cardinals, and not just in the managerial seat. In mid-August, Claiborne was dismissed as general manager; he was replaced by Herzog, who turned the lineup card over to coach Red Schoendienst, who ran the team for its last 37 games. In October, Herzog was named general manager–manager.

The arrangement was perfect for a man who did not want to spend all his time sitting in an office but who wanted to exercise control over the character and makeup of the club. In his autobiography *White Rat* (a nickname he likes), Herzog gives some insight into the dictates of his thinking:

> In baseball today, geography is all-important. In the National League, you've got a whole bunch of big ballparks—ten, to be exact— where it's hard to hit home runs. Our park in St. Louis, where we play eighty-one games a year, is the toughest hitter's park of them all.

With this in mind, Herzog set out to build a team whose strength was speed, pitching (in-

Keith Hernandez making contact.

cluding a strong bullpen), defense, and a catcher who could throw. Armed with the knowledge of a manager, the authority of a general manager, and the backing of August Busch, Whitey went to baseball's winter meetings in December and turned these often talky but inconclusive gatherings inside out and upside down.

On December 8, Whitey acquired from San Diego relief ace Rollie Fingers, left-hander Bob Shirley, catcher Gene Tenace, and minor league catcher Bob Geren. The Cardinals gave up catchers Steve Swisher and Terry Kennedy, infielder Mike Phillips, and pitchers John Littlefield, John Urrea, Kim Seaman, and Alan Olmstead.

Infielder Ken Oberkfell (1977–84), who batted over .300 in 1979 and 1980.

204

The following day, Herzog obtained another top reliever from the Cubs, Bruce Sutter, in exchange for first baseman–outfielder Leon Durham, third baseman Ken Reitz, and infielder Ty Waller.

The Cardinals now possessed what many people consider are the two top relievers of all time. Herzog suddenly had what he described as "the greatest bullpen in the history of the world." But he also knew it was one stopper too many: Sutter and Fingers were simply too talented to be able to coexist in the same pen. Each was accustomed to the closer's role and Whitey knew it would be impossible to juggle them and keep both happy.

So on December 12, Herzog swung another crowded deal—Fingers, right-hander Pete Vuckovich, and Ted Simmons to Milwaukee for outfielders Sixto Lezcano and David Green and pitchers Lary Sorensen and Dave LaPoint. This deal brought prosperity to the Brewers—Fingers

Bruce Sutter (1981–84), who led the league on saves in each of his four years in St. Louis.

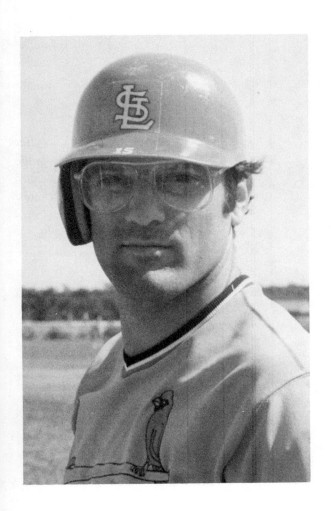

in 1981 and Vuckovich in 1982 each won Cy Young Awards, with the Brewers winning the pennant in the latter year. Simmons was replaced behind the plate by Darrell Porter, who had caught for Herzog in Kansas City and whose free-agency signing was announced on December 13. (Though Simmons's bat would be missed, his slowness afoot and weak throwing arm had disenchanted Herzog.)

In less than a week, Herzog had unloaded thirteen players and added nine. In so doing he had begun reshaping the team to emphasize the speed, defense, and pitching he felt were needed

Catcher Darrell Porter (1981–85).

Utility infielder Dane Iorg (1977–84). He had nine hits and a .529 batting average in the 1982 World Series.

postseason in front of their television sets (as did the team with the best record in the West, the Cincinnati Reds).

Dane Iorg led the Redbirds with a .327 average and Hernandez was at .306. Switch-hitting Tommy Herr, a hustling, heads-up player, was now installed at second base. Forsch led the staff with a 10–5 record. Posting a 6–1 mark after being obtained in a June 7 deal with Houston was the talented and temperamental Joaquin Andujar. Sutter was everything Herzog knew he would be, logging a league-leading 25 saves in the abbreviated season.

After the season, Herzog began dealing again. The trade he made on October 21, 1981, was not a headline-grabber by any means; it was the sort of deal that makes the "Transactions" column and is quickly forgotten—a marginal pitcher for a minor leaguer. The pitcher was lefty Bob Sykes, who was 2–0 for the

to win in Busch Stadium and around the rest of the National League.

The initial implementation of Whitey's "grand design" was interrupted by the season-shattering players' strike of 1981 that cut the middle third out of the schedule. When play was resumed in early August, it was decided to divide the season into two halves, with the respective winners meeting in postseason play to determine division winners before a second round of playoffs to crown a pennant winner.

This peculiar arrangement turned out to be unfortunate for the Cardinals. Herzog's team posted the best full-season record in the Eastern Division—59–43—but were a game-and-a-half out when the strike was called (trailing Philadelphia) and then a half game out in the second half (trailing Montreal). So the team with the best overall record in their division spent the

Second baseman Tommy Herr (1979–88).

That's Keith Hernandez sliding home safely past Pittsburgh's
Tony Peña. The action took place at Pittsburgh's Three Rivers Stadium in August 1982.

Cardinals in 1981, and the minor leaguer was Yankee farmhand Willie McGee.

In November the Cardinals were involved in a three-way deal with Cleveland and Philadelphia in which they parted with pitchers Lary Sorensen and Silvio Martinez and came away with outfielder Lonnie Smith.

In December there was a six-man swap with the Padres, the principals being shortstops Garry Templeton and Ozzie Smith.

"Ozzie is not only the greatest defensive shortstop ever to play the game," Herzog said, "but he's also a first-rate human being, a leader in the best sense of the word."

Smith, whose coverage of shortstop threatened to wear out the word "spectacular," had reflexes of feline quickness, a strong arm, and moves in the face of sliding runners that were nothing less than acrobatic. It was "The Wizardry of Oz" at shortstop, and Smith became known as "The Wizard." When he joined the Cardinals he was twenty-seven years old, a four-year man who had batted .222 the year before.

Uncomfortable with sitting in an office all winter (when he could have been out hunting or fishing), Herzog gave up the general manager's job to his assistant Joe McDonald and

Outfielder Lonnie Smith (1982–85) at New York's Shea Stadium. He was a .321 hitter in 1983.

concentrated full time on winning the pennant in 1982.

The key to the Cardinals' success in 1982 was consistency—they never lost more than three games in a row until after they had clinched the pennant. They asserted themselves with a 12-game winning streak in April, played steadily throughout the season, and then broke apart a close race with an eight-game winning streak in mid-September and finally locked up the division on September 27. Their margin at the end was three games over the Phillies. St. Louis fans demonstrated their ap-

preciation for this first victory in 14 years by setting a new club attendance record—2,111,906.

The team hit just 67 home runs (leading Herzog to wonder at one point during the season whether the team would break Maris's record) and became the first division winner ever to finish last in the major leagues in home runs.

But Herzog had not designed his team to hit home runs: What he wanted was the old Cardinal formula for success—speed, defense, and pitching. The Redbirds led with 200 stolen bases, including 68 by Lonnie Smith, and they led in defense with a .981 mark, while their adequate starting pitching was supported by the concrete pillar that was Bruce Sutter's right arm. The champion reliever won nine and saved a league-leading 36. The top winners were Forsch (15–9) and Andujar (15–10).

Lonnie Smith, who finished second in the MVP voting to Atlanta's Dale Murphy, led the club with a .307 average, with Hernandez, McGee, Oberkfell, and Hendrick all over .280. Hendrick, with 19 homers and 109 RBIs, was the team's big gun.

The Cardinals ran over the Braves in the playoffs (still a best-of-five series then) in three straight, with Forsch setting the tone with a three-hit shutout in the opener and Sutter saving the next two by retiring every one of the 13 men he faced.

Opposing the Cardinals in the World Series were Harvey Kuenn's hard-hitting Milwaukee Brewers—"Harvey's Wallbangers," who had cracked 216 home runs, more than three times as many as the exponents of "Whitey Ball." Kuenn's lineup bulged with the bats of Gorman Thomas, Robin Yount, Paul Molitor, Ben Oglivie, Cecil Cooper, Jim Gantner, and a familiar name, Ted Simmons. Ex-Cardinal Pete Vuckovich led the Brewer staff. The Cardinals received a break when Milwaukee's star reliever Rollie Fingers was forced out of the Series with an aching elbow.

The Cardinals followed what had almost become an October tradition for them—the seven-game World Series. It was their eighth in 13 visits to the October extravaganza.

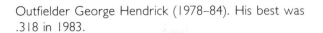

Outfielder George Hendrick (1978–84). His best was .318 in 1983.

The first two games in St. Louis were divided, Milwaukee roaring to a 10–0 win in the opener and then the Cardinals prevailing 5–4, with Sutter getting the victory.

In Game 3 at Milwaukee, it was St. Louis by a 6–2 score. Andujar pitched six-and-a-third scoreless innings before being hit on the knee by a line drive. The bullpen, with Sutter getting the save, finished up. Willie McGee, with only four home runs all season, suddenly turned lethal, hitting a three-run shot in the fifth and a solo blow in the seventh.

1982 World Series action: Ozzie Smith, having just forced Milwaukee's Jim Gantner at second, is firing on to first to complete the double play. The play took place in the sixth inning of Game 3.

The Brewers evened it up by taking Game 4, 7–5, then went ahead three games to two with a 6–4 win the next day. So the Series returned to St. Louis, with the Cardinals, as they had been in their championship years of 1926, 1934, and 1946, finding themselves being squeezed toward oblivion.

In Game 6, right-hander John Stuper, 9–7 for the season, went all the way in a Redbird romp, 13–1.

The starters for Game 7 were Vuckovich and Andujar. The Brewers took a 3–1 lead into the bottom of the sixth. The Cardinals loaded the bases with none out and had Hernandez coming to the plate. One of the Series' sidebar stories, Hernandez had gone 0-for-15 during the first four games, then 7-for-12 in the last three, with his biggest hit coming right now—a game-

Outfield larceny in the ninth inning of Game 3 of the 1982 World Series. That's Willie McGee robbing Milwaukee's Gorman Thomas of a probable home run. Willie also hit two home runs in the game.

The volatile Joaquin Andujar is going after Jim Gantner after exchanging some heated words with the Milwaukee player during the seventh game of the 1982 World Series. Umpire Bill Haller is throwing an effective block.

The Cardinals have just won the 1982 World Series and Darrell Porter is congratulating Bruce Sutter, who shut down the Milwaukee Brewers in the final innings of Game 7.

the afterglow of a world title lured 2,343,716 customers into Busch Stadium, a new Cardinal record.

Eight-game losing streaks in June and August and a seven-game plunge in September leaked just enough glue into the Cardinal gears to keep them from moving with any speed.

On June 15, 1983, Cardinal fans learned of a stunning trade involving one of their star players. Keith Hernandez had been swapped to the Mets for right-handers Neil Allen and Rick Ownbey. Herzog's explanation was that these were two highly talented young pitchers who would help the club. While Whitey believed this to be true, the full story covered a little more ground. Hernandez, in the skipper's opin-

The Cardinals celebrating after the final out of the 1982 Series.

tying two-run single to right-center. Hendrick then singled in what proved to be the winning run as St. Louis, with the inevitable Sutter on the mound at the end, took their ninth world title, the final score 6–3.

There was no repeat performance for the Cardinals in 1983; in fact, they fell to fourth place, 11 games behind, despite some substantial hitting by Herr (.323), Lonnie Smith (.321), and Hendrick (.318). The club set a new franchise record with 207 stolen bases, Bob Forsch became the first Cardinal to pitch two no-hitters when he stopped Montreal on September 26, 3–0, and the élan of Whitey's boys along with

Left-hander Jim Kaat (1980–83), who finished up his 25-year big-league career with St. Louis.

6–16 season in 1983 to lead the league in wins (20–14) and had Sutter tie the major league record with 45 saves. But the hitting just wasn't there this year and it took a 17–13 September to get them into third place.

The highlight of the year, as far as Herzog was concerned, was the emergence of Terry Pendleton. After trying Andy Van Slyke at third and not being satisfied, Herzog put Andy back in the outfield and brought up the switch-hitting Pendleton (who, along with Ozzie Smith, McGee, and Herr, gave the club four switch-hitters). Terry made himself at home immediately, covering the position smoothly and batting .324 in 67 games.

To make a sluggish year even worse, after the season the Cardinals lost Bruce Sutter to a free-agency signing with Atlanta. Losing his bullpen ace was a heavy blow to Herzog, who said, "My whole team was the preliminary act to Bruce Sutter's show-stopper, and the whole world knew it."

ion, had "an attitude problem." Herzog felt that Keith, while playing a brilliant first base, had been loafing on offense—not running out ground balls and not being aggressive on the bases. Afraid that Hernandez's casual approach might contaminate the rest of the club, Herzog convinced ownership to make the deal.

Though he was 10–6 for the Cardinals that year, Allen never panned out in St. Louis, nor did Ownbey. To replace Hernandez at first base, Herzog moved George Hendrick in from the outfield and to fill Hendrick's spot brought up Andy Van Slyke, a ballplayer who was going to just get better and better.

The 1984 Cardinals did a lot of the things that Herzog wanted them to do—they led the league with 220 stolen bases (a new club high), made the fewest errors (118), most double plays (184), and had the best fielding percentage (.982). They also had Andujar rebound from a

Outfielder Andy Van Slyke (1983–86), who was traded to Pittsburgh in 1987 for catcher Tony Peña.

The excitable but talented Joaquin Andujar (1981–85). He was a twenty-game winner for the Cards in 1984 and 1985.

Slick-fielding third baseman Terry Pendleton, who joined the Cardinals in 1984.

John Tudor (1985–87, 1990), who was 21–8 in 1985.

Jack Clark (1985–87).

The loss of Sutter led to dire prophecies for the Cardinals in 1985. How could a club expect to contend after losing the game's top relief pitcher, a man who had saved 45 games? Most preseason forecasters saw St. Louis finishing deep in the division. But by the time the season was over, the Redbirds were baseball's "surprise team," winners in the Eastern Division by three games over a tough New York Mets team that won 98 games to the Cardinals' 101.

With Dal Maxvill, formerly an infielder with the club, now in the general manager's job, the Cardinals had swung two crucial off-season deals. On December 12, 1984, they obtained left-hander John Tudor from the Pirates for Hendrick (whose best days were behind him), and then on February 1, 1985, a transaction with the Giants brought them the power-hitting Jack Clark in exchange for shortstop Jose Uribe, outfielders David Green and Gary Rajsich, and lefty Dave LaPoint.

Very early in the season, some minor injuries in the outfield necessitated the recall of minor leaguer Vince Coleman.

"It'll be only for a week or so," Maxvill told him.

It turned out to be a very long week. The addition to the lineup of Coleman—a flash of lightning on the bases—gave Herzog five switch-hitters on the card, limiting or nullifying the moves an opposing manager could make with his bullpen.

Led by Coleman's 100 steals (a record for rookies; he was caught 25 times), the Cardinals stole a team-record 314 bases. McGee had 56, and Herr, Van Slyke, and Ozzie Smith over 30 each. With Coleman and McGee at the top of the lineup, getting on base and burning up the paths, Tommy Herr, batting third, had the year of his life, batting .302 and driving in 110 runs. Clark hit 22 home runs and drove in 87 runs despite missing the final six weeks of the season with an injured rib cage.

When Clark was sidelined, Maxvill reached out and acquired from Cincinnati the veteran Cesar Cedeño, once one of the league's top players, but now measuring out his days as a backup man for the Reds. Taking over at first

Vince Coleman, who stole more than 100 bases in each of his first three big-league seasons.

base, the thirty-four-year-old Cedeño went on a tear for St. Louis, breaking into 28 games and batting .434.

The MVP designation went to McGee, who put together a blazing year, winning the batting crown (.353, highest ever for a National League switch-hitter), as well as leading in hits (216) and triples (18). Coleman was unanimous choice for Rookie of the Year.

Smith and Pendleton sealed up the left side of the infield and McGee, Coleman, and Van

The infield of the 1985 National League pennant winners. *Left to right:* Terry Pendleton, Ozzie Smith, Tommy Herr, and Jack Clark.

Slyke constituted what Herzog said "might be the best defensive outfield in the history of the game." Overall, Cardinal leather was the most efficient in the league, posting a .983 fielding percentage, based on 108 errors, which were the best figures in the league and the best in team history.

For John Tudor it was a night-and-day season. The taciturn left-hander started off by losing seven of his first eight decisions, then made a stunning turnaround by winning 20 of his last 21, and doing it with consistent brilliance. Along with his 21–8 record were a league-high ten shutouts and 1.93 ERA, second best in the league to Dwight Gooden's 1.53.

Andujar was 21–12, and in some respects his season resembled Tudor's, though in reverse: the excitable right-hander won his 20th game on August 23 and then only one more after that. Herzog's third big winner was something of a surprise. After going 9–11 in 1984,

Willie McGee, who was MVP and batting champion in 1985.

Right-hander Danny Cox, an 18-game winner in 1985.

Left-hander Ricky Horton (1984–87), who started and relieved, helping the Cardinals to two pennants.

Right-hander Jeff Lahti (1982–86), who did some excellent bullpen work for the Redbirds before going down with an arm injury.

big right-hander Danny Cox turned in an 18–9 record.

It took a "bullpen by committee" to replace Sutter, but this was a committee that worked smoothly. Herzog juggled right-handers Bill Campbell and Jeff Lahti (the leader with 19 saves) and lefties Ricky Horton and Ken Dayley, and toward the end of the season added Todd Worrell, a big right-hander with a 98-miles-per-hour fastball. The "committee" logged 44 saves, one fewer than Sutter had in 1984, and enough to get the job done—the team was 83-1 in games they led after seven innings.

The division wasn't settled until the last few days of the season. The Mets came into St. Louis for a three-game series trailing by three. New York took the first two to tighten it up, but then Cox beat them 4–3 in what was the season's key game. Two days later, Tudor clinched it with a 7–1 win over the Cubs.

The Cardinals met the Los Angeles Dodgers

Ken Dayley, a key member of Whitey Herzog's
"bullpen by committee."

"The Wizard," Ozzie Smith, possibly
the greatest defensive shortstop of all time.

in the pennant playoffs, now a best-of-seven affair. Opening in Los Angeles, the series started off dismally for St. Louis, as Tom Lasorda's club won the first two games, beating Tudor and Andujar.

Back home, the Cardinals won Game 3 behind Cox and three members of the "committee," 4–2. The next day, the club treated Tudor to a nine-run second inning and an easy 12–2 win, knotting the series at two games apiece. After that, the Cardinals resorted to their "secret weapon"—the home run, which they had kept concealed all season (their 87 homers ranked them 25th among the 26 big-league teams in 1985).

The fifth game was tied 2–2 in the bottom of the ninth inning when Ozzie Smith came to the plate and demonstrated one of baseball's eternal enchantments—the wondrously unexpected. With one out and no one on base, Smith stunned the Dodgers, the St. Louis fans, and most of the universe of baseball by lining one of reliever Tom Niedenfuer's fastballs off one of the concrete pillars above the right-field wall for a home run. Ozzie, who had once gone three straight years without hitting a bell-ringer, had hit only 13 in his eight big-league seasons—and none of them from the left side of the plate. (As if to emphasize how unique his blow was, Ozzie went homerless the next two seasons.)

The Cardinals had now won three straight and as they journeyed back to Los Angeles needed just one more to put the wrap on the pennant. Game 6 matched Andujar against Orel Hershiser, but by the time the game reached the ninth inning it was Worrell against Niedenfuer. Herzog's men came to bat in the top of the ninth trailing 5–4.

With one out, McGee singled, then stole second. Ozzie Smith walked. Herr rolled out to the first baseman, advancing the runners to second and third. It was now two out and the batter was Jack Clark, in Herzog's estimation "the best clutch fastball hitter in baseball." Niedenfuer, like most closers, was a fastball pitcher.

The question for Lasorda was whether to walk Clark and then bring in a left-handed re-

liever to face Andy Van Slyke (for whom Herzog later said he would have pinch-hit the seldom-used Brian Harper), or pitch to Clark. Lasorda opted for the latter, for which he has been severely second-guessed. The Dodger skipper's move was not without some logic, however. For one thing, loading the bases puts added pressure on a pitcher to throw strikes to the next batter, and sometimes the tendency is to make those strikes a bit too lush. For another thing, Lasorda had his stopper on the mound, the man who had done the job for him all year.

Niedenfuer threw one pitch to Clark and for the second game in a row the St. Louis "secret weapon" struck, albeit this time from a more likely source. Clark ripped a screamer high into the left-field pavilion, putting the Cardinals up, 7–5. Ken Dayley blew away the Dodgers in the bottom of the ninth and the Cardinals had won their 13th pennant, thanks to the most resounding Redbird home run since the one that Whitey Kurowski struck against the Yankees to win the 1942 World Series.

The 1985 World Series was dubbed "The I-70 Series" for the ribbon of interstate highway that linked the two Missouri-based contestants, the Cardinals and the Kansas City Royals, who were led by one of the era's great hitters, George Brett.

The Series opened in Kansas City with a Cardinal victory, Tudor winning, 3–1. Game 2 was a duel between Cox and lefty Charley Leibrandt. With the Royals up by a 2–0 score in the top of the ninth, the Cardinals suddenly mounted a rally. McGee opened with a double, followed by two outs. Clark then singled Willie home, making it 2–1. Tito Landrum then blooped a double to right, sending Clark to third. (Landrum was playing because Vince Coleman had been injured in a bizarre accident during the playoffs when a mechanically operated tarpaulin knocked him down and ran over his leg.)

At this point Cedeño was walked intentionally, filling the bases. Terry Pendleton then cleared them with a double down the left-field line, giving the Cardinals a 4–2 lead, which Jeff Lahti protected in the bottom of the ninth.

It's the fifth inning of Game 1 of the 1985 World Series between the Cardinals and the Kansas City Royals, and Willie McGee is about to be tagged out at third on a textbook relay from center fielder Willie Wilson to second baseman Frank White to third baseman George Brett. McGee was caught trying to stretch a double into a triple. Hal Lanier is the third-base coach.

The Series then moved to Busch Stadium, where Royals ace Bret Saberhagen defeated Andujar, 6–1. The next day Tudor gave the Redbirds a commanding three-games-to-one bulge with a masterful five-hitter, 3–0.

The Royals, who had been down 3–1 to Toronto in their pennant playoffs and rebounded to victory, now found themselves in the same predicament, and once more they began digging their way out of the hole.

Kansas City got to Bob Forsch early in Game

5 and went on to a 6–1 win behind lefty Danny Jackson. (Worrell, in relief, struck out all six batters he faced.) The Series then returned to Kansas City and a most controversial Game 6.

For seven innings Cox and Leibrandt matched each other with scoreless innings. In the top of the eighth, pinch-hitter Brian Harper blooped a single to center, scoring Pendleton and giving the Cardinals a 1–0 lead.

The game went into the bottom of the

(TOP LEFT) Outfielder Tito Landrum (1980–87).

(TOP RIGHT) Vince Coleman on the move. Run over by an automatic tarpaulin, Coleman missed action in the 1985 Series.

(LEFT) Tommy Herr forcing George Brett at second in a bit of byplay from the '85 Series.

ninth, St. Louis leading by that one run and Worrell on the mound now. The first man he faced was pinch-hitter Jorge Orta. Orta bounced a chopper to the right side that was fielded by Clark, who tossed to Worrell covering. Umpire Don Denkinger called Orta safe, though television replays showed the runner was clearly out. Denkinger had muffed the call and Herzog's vehement protest was in vain.

The Royals received another break when the next batter, Steve Balboni, lifted a playable pop foul near the first-base dugout that fell untouched. Balboni then converted the "life" into a single to left, sending Orta to second. Attempting to sacrifice, Jim Sundberg bunted into a force at third, Worrell making a fine play.

At this point, catcher Darrell Porter committed a passed ball, allowing the runners to move up to second and third. Hal McRae was then intentionally walked to fill the bases. Kansas City skipper Dick Howser then sent up ex-Cardinal Dane Iorg to pinch-hit, and Iorg rifled a hit to right that scored the tying and winning runs. It was the first time all year that the Cardinals had lost a game in the ninth inning.

The bottom of that ninth inning of Game 6 was a twisted series of blunders and mishaps, from Denkinger's errant call to the untouched pop foul to the passed ball, that cost the Cardinals the game and the World Championship. True, there was a seventh game, but it was Kansas City and Bret Saberhagen all the way—11–0. The Royals tore the game apart in the bottom of the fifth when they added six runs to the 5–0 lead they already had, an inning that saw Cardinal frustrations rise with the score. During that inning, which seemed like an eternity to the Cardinals, both Herzog and Andujar were ejected for arguing with the plate umpire, who happened to be Don Denkinger.

The barely missed world title left some bitterness, but it took the always realistic Herzog to remind people that a team some experts had picked to finish last had won 101 games and the pennant, drawn 2,637,563 customers, and made it to the seventh game of the World Series.

"I'll take that every year," Whitey said.

The 1980s were proving to be a difficult time for winners seeking to repeat, and in 1986 the Cardinals became the latest club to languish under this syndrome. Herzog's club finished third, and did that well only because of a strong second half. The combination of a sluggish start in St. Louis and a greyhound getaway in New York by a Mets team that eventually won 108 games and the division by 21½ soured the summer for the Cardinals and the rest of the division.

The Cardinals' offensive decline was precipitous. After leading the league in batting (.264) and runs (747) in 1985, a year later they were last in the major leagues in batting (.236), runs (601), and home runs (58).

McGee dropped 97 points to .256, Herr melted down by 50 points to .252, Coleman

Todd Worrell, Rookie of the Year in 1986 and Herzog's top man in the bullpen.

fell from .267 to .232 (though leading in stolen bases with 107 in 121 attempts), and Clark was lost for the season on June 24 when he suffered torn ligaments in his thumb.

With Andujar having been traded to Oakland, Forsch was the top winner with a 14–10 ledger, though Tudor led the staff in efficiency at 13–7. Worrell was a dominant force in relief, winning nine and leading the league with 36 saves. Having pitched only 22 innings in 1985, he was still considered a rookie in 1986, making him eligible for the Rookie of the Year designation, which he indeed won, the fifth Cardinal to have been so cited. Another freshman, left-hander Greg Mathews, was 11–8.

The Cardinals came back in 1987 to take a division title, a victory so unexpected that it surprised even Herzog. The preseason forecasters assumed the Mets were unbeatable and ceded them the title before a ball was thrown. The talented Mets pitching staff, however, began checking onto the disabled list with various hurts and misfortunes, forcing the New Yorkers to come back to the rest of the division.

The Cardinals were not without some injuries of their own. Catcher Tony Peña, acquired from the Pirates in a spring trade for Van Slyke, pitcher Mike Dunne, and catcher Mike La Valliere, suffered a broken thumb in the third game of the season and was out for six weeks. Soon after, in one of the most freakish of accidents, Tudor had a bone broken in his leg when Mets catcher Barry Lyons crashed into him in the dugout in pursuit of a pop foul. Tudor was out until August 1. On September 9, Clark suffered a season-ending ankle sprain.

In spite of injuries and a lack of frontline pitching, St. Louis played winning ball and by July 23 had built up a lead of 9½ games over Montreal and 10½ over the Mets. The Redbirds then lost seven in a row, including three to the Mets, and the complexion of the race began to change.

On September 11, Herzog brought his team into New York for a key three-game series after having just lost three straight to Montreal and seeing their lead over the Mets cut to 1½. Going into the top of the ninth inning of the

Tony Peña giving the "thumbs up" sign.

opener, the Mets were winning, 4–2. With two out, McGee singled, and then Pendleton belted St. Louis's "biggest hit of the year," a two-run homer that tied the score. The Cardinals won it in the tenth, split the remain-

The versatile Jose Oquendo. Name the position, he'll play it.

ing two games, and from there went on to take the division title, clinching in their 159th game.

Despite hitting the fewest home runs in the league—94, with 35 of them by Clark (who set a team record with 136 walks)—Herzog fielded a lineup of steady hitters. Smith led the club with his highest average ever, .303, Coleman was at .289, Pendleton and Clark .286, and McGee .285. Part-time outfielder Curt Ford gave Whitey a .285 season and all-purpose man Jose Oquendo, who started at seven different positions during the season, batted. 286. With 109 stolen bases, Coleman became the first ever to steal more than 100 bags three years in a row. The team's 248 successful thefts gave them the league lead for the sixth straight year.

This consistent offense supported a division-winning staff that, remarkably, saw no one win more than 11 games. Forsch, Cox, and Mathews were the modestly achieving toppers, while Tudor, who missed much of the season, was 10–2. Worrell, with 33 saves and a club-record 75 appearances, headed a bullpen corps that included some excellent work by Ken Dayley and Ricky Horton.

The Cardinals' fine season (95–67) did not go unnoticed or unappreciated by their fans, who came out often enough to set a new and most impressive club attendance record—3,072,122, an average of nearly 38,000 per game.

For the third time the Cardinals went into a pennant playoff and for the third time they won. Their opponents this time were the San Francisco Giants, a team that blasted 205 home runs during the regular season and who would out-homer the Cardinals nine to two during the seven-game series.

The teams split the first two games, played in St. Louis, Mathews winning 5–3 and then Tudor suffering a 5–0 shutout at the hands of Dave Dravecky. The series then moved to Candlestick Park and there the Cardinals took the third game, 6–5. The Giants evened it up once more with a 4–2 victory in Game 4 and the following day went a leg up with a 6–3 win.

The two contenders returned to St. Louis to complete the series, and at this point Cardinal pitching sealed the hatches. In Game 6, Tudor, with late-inning help from Worrell and Dayley, shut out the Giants, 1–0. The lone run came in the second inning on Tony Peña's triple, which right-fielder Candy Maldonado lost in the lights, and Oquendo's sacrifice fly.

Danny Cox and Atlee Hammaker were the starting pitchers for the decisive seventh game. The Cardinals broke loose with four runs in the bottom of the second, thanks to a power display from a man who in terms of power had always been a twenty-watt bulb—Jose Oquendo. After three singles had given the Redbirds a run, up stepped Oquendo, a man who in 903 big-league at bats had hit just two home runs. The Cardinals' sterling all-purpose man startled the Giants, the Cardinals, 55,331 Busch Stadium patrons, and a vast television audience when he rapped a Hammaker delivery over the left-field wall for a three-run homer.

Cox now had more than he would need as he went on to pitch a six-hit, 6–0 shutout and give the Cardinals their 15th National League pennant. St. Louis pitching closed out the series with 23 straight scoreless innings.

Exponents of the seven-game World Series, the Cardinals went the distance once again that October, for the tenth time. The Series was played to a peculiar pattern—the home team won every time. Unfortunately for the Cardinals, four of the seven games were played on the home field of their opponents, the Minnesota Twins. (The Twins' primacy on their home grounds should not have come as any surprise, for during the regular season they were 56–25 at the enclosed Hubert H. Humphrey Metrodome.)

The Twins made it easy in the first two games, using a seven-run fourth inning to rout starter Joe Magrane 10–1 in the opener and then a six-run fourth inning to kayo Cox and go on to an 8–4 win in Game 2.

With the Series moving to St. Louis for three games, home cooking continued to prevail. Tudor put the Redbirds back into things with a 3–1 victory, the Cardinals scoring all their runs in the last of the seventh, with Coleman's two-run single being the big hit.

Twice the Twins had used the last half of the fourth inning to break open a game, and now it was the Cardinals' turn. Herzog's men used this half inning in Game 4 to score six times. The outburst was marked by another Cardinal home run from a most unlikely source. Tom Lawless, who with just 25 at bats all season was the personification of the bench-warmer, was playing third base in place of a hobbled Terry Pendleton. To the astonishment of one and all, Lawless parked a three-run crasher in this inning, and to the amusement of many he flipped his bat nonchalantly into the air, an act that belied his own disbelief in what he had just done, and began his home

Greg Mathews, St. Louis's talented but injury-ridden southpaw.

Tom Lawless has just stunned Minnesota's Frank Viola (left) and the rest of the universe of baseball with a three-run homer in the fourth inning of Game 4 of the 1987 World Series. Catcher Tim Laudner and umpire John McSherry are watching it fly.

run trot looking as though he was bored by the routine (his previous big-league home run had come in 1984). The final score was 4–2, with Forsch getting the win.

Behind the strong pitching of Cox, who was picked up by Dayley and Worrell in the late innings, the Cardinals took Game 5, 4–2, with another improbable hero, Curt Ford, drilling a key two-run single in a three-run Cardinal sixth.

The Series then returned to Minnesota. Going into the bottom of the fifth in Game 6, the Cardinals held a 5–2 lead, with Tudor pitching. But then the Twins put together back-to-back four-run innings and went on to an 11–5 win, sending the affair into what for St. Louis was familiar territory—a seventh game.

The be-all and end-all game of the 1987 baseball season was played in front of more than 55,000 fans, whose unrelenting cheering created within the domed stadium an incredible amount of noise. The starters were Magrane and for the Twins Frank Viola, their ace lefty, who had thus far split two decisions in the Series. St. Louis got off to a 2–0 lead in the top of the second, but those were the last runs they would score in 1987. The Twins began pecking away at Magrane, then at Cox, then at Worrell. When it was over, Minnesota had a 4–2 victory and its first World Championship.

For a team looking forward to repeating in 1988, the new year did not break promisingly for St. Louis. Clark had played out the last year of his contract and the club and the slugger were unable to come to terms on a new pact. On January 6, it was announced that the man who had been the team's big buster for the past three years had signed with the New York Yankees as a free agent. Trying to fill this enormous gap in their lineup, the Cardinals a week later signed free-agent Bob Horner, one-time Atlanta Braves power hitter who had spent the 1987 season playing in Japan. Horner's career had been gouged by injuries and his service with the Cardinals followed this pattern—on June 20 a serious shoulder injury sidelined him for the season.

The Cardinals opened their defense of their division title by losing 12 of their first 16. By early June they had played themselves back into contention and trailed the front-running Mets by 6½. But then came a disastrous slide—

34 losses in 47 games. By the time Herzog got the engines going again in August, the club was on its way to a lackluster fifth-place finish.

The pitching staff was crippled by a series of injuries and ailments throughout the summer. Danny Cox and Greg Mathews each were limited to 13 starts, Tudor missed the first three weeks of the season recovering from off-season shoulder surgery, and Dayley tore a back muscle on opening day and labored through much of the season. Joe Magrane, the team's opening-day pitcher, also had the miseries, putting in two months on the disabled list and finishing with a 5–9 record. When he was in there, however, the big left-hander was effective enough to log a 2.18 ERA, best in the league. Magrane had the dubious distinction of having the fewest wins ever for an ERA leader.

It's the sixth inning of Game 7 of the 1987 World Series. Tommy Herr is clearly safe getting back to first base on a rundown. But umpire Lee Weyer, who seems blocked by first baseman Kent Hrbek, called Herr out. Minnesota pitcher Frank Viola is reaching to make the tag.

Left-hander Joe Magrane, an ERA leader despite just five victories.

Though hitting just .245, "Bruno" led the club with 22 home runs and 79 runs batted in. On August 16, Tudor (who was just 6–5) was dealt to Los Angeles for the heavy-hitting Pedro Guerrero, who was slowed by injuries but who still swung a potent bat.

"Super sub" Jose Oquendo filled in at second for Herr, at third when Pendleton missed 50 games with injuries, and put in time at every other position, including one game behind the plate and four innings on the mound, making him the first Cardinal since Gene Paulette in 1918 to appear at all nine positions.

Despite their stop-and-go season, the Cardinals continued to draw enormous crowds,

On the positive side was the performance of Jose DeLeon. Acquired from the Chicago White Sox for Ricky Horton, the hard-throwing right-hander was the ace with a 13–10 record and 208 strikeouts, the first Redbird since Gibson in 1972 to fan more than 200. Worrell carried the bullpen with 32 saves.

McGee led the club with a .292 average, but his RBIs dropped from 105 to 50. Coleman failed to reach 100 stolen bases for the first time, though his 81 were good enough to lead the league.

Two significant trades were made during the season. On the hunt for power, the club on April 22 traded bulwark second baseman Tommy Herr to their 1987 World Series opponents for longballer Tom Brunansky.

Right-hander Jose DeLeon, who had 208 strikeouts in 1988.

Scott Terry, who started his career as an outfielder in the Cincinnati organization.

Dal Maxvill: from shortstop to general manager.

Tom Brunansky, who came to St. Louis in 1988 in a trade for Tommy Herr.

Pedro Guerrero, a .300 hitter with genuine sock. The Cardinals traded John Tudor to Los Angeles to get him.

compiling a total attendance of 2,892,629, proving once again they were the heart of baseball in the heart of America.

Any team managed by Whitey Herzog was automatically considered a contender, and so the Cardinals went into the 1989 season with high hopes. With Peña behind the plate and an infield of Guerrero at first, Oquendo at second, Smith at short, and Pendleton at third, and Coleman, McGee, and Brunansky in the outfield, the regular lineup was a strong one. The starters—and here some fingers were crossed—would be selected from among DeLeon, Magrane, Terry, rookie Ken Hill, Cox, and Mathews.

The bad news, however, began coming early. In mid-March it was announced that Cox would have to undergo elbow surgery that would take him out of the picture for the entire season. Then, soon after the schedule got underway, Mathews was similarly sidelined for the rest of the year after surgery to repair ligament damage in his left elbow.

The good news from the mound was provided by DeLeon and Magrane. For years they had been saying about DeLeon, "He's got great stuff, but he never wins." In 1989, however, he began revising that summation, winning five of his first six decisions and going on to a 16–12 record and a league-leading 201 strikeouts.

Magrane, after a slow start, began winning big. Herzog spotted the improvement early, saying in May, "Joe is going to be a Cy Young contender." Though Magrane did not win the award, he indeed made a prophet of his skipper by going on to a fine 18–9 season, with a 2.91 ERA.

Hill disappointed with a 7–15 record, while Terry was 8–10. With Worrell and Dayley in the pen, the relief pitching was strong, strong enough for middle reliever Frank DiPino to post a 9–0 record.

With the exception of McGee, who was limited to 58 games in an injury-riddled season, the St. Louis regulars were a hardy bunch in 1989. Guerrero, Oquendo, Smith, Pendleton, Brunansky, and Milt Thompson each played in 155 or more games, a showing not equaled

Todd Zeile, the Cardinals' "catcher of the future."

by any team in the league. With McGee hurt, Thompson took over in center and played well, batting .290. (Thompson had been acquired in an off-season trade with the Phillies for Steve Lake and Curt Ford.)

No team was able to dominate the National League East in 1989, with four teams—St. Louis, New York, Montreal, and Chicago—in equal contention. At the All-Star break the Cardinals were in fourth place, just three games

Ozzie Smith: The Wizard in action.

out. The Cubs took over the top spot on August 7 and, though no one suspected it at the time, would remain there. The Cardinals hung tough and as late as September 8 were but a half game behind. But then they began a fatal five-game slide that gradually took them out of the race.

The key to his team's September decline, Herzog felt, was the loss early in the month of Worrell to a bad elbow. With their top closer unavailable to weld shut late-inning leads, the Cardinals were vulnerable. At the end, St. Louis was in third place, seven games behind the Cubs.

Along with the strong pitching of DeLeon and Magrane, the club had some other high achievers in 1989. Although his stolen base total dropped to 65, it was good enough for Coleman to lead the league for the fifth straight time. At one point, the Cardinal speed wheel ran off a new major league record, 50 consec-utive steals (the first six dating to the end of the 1988 season), before being thrown out by Montreal's Nelson Santovenia on July 28.

In his first full season in a Cardinal uniform, Guerrero turned in some handsome stick work, batting .311 and driving in 117 runs. Oquendo batted .291, including a 23-game hitting streak, and Smith once again flashed and dazzled at shortstop, winning another Gold Glove that gave him the distinction of having taken the award every year of the 1980s.

Toward the end of the season, the Cardinals began breaking in twenty-four-year-old Todd Zeile, who was considered the team's "catcher of the future." In 28 games, Zeile batted .256 and impressed the organization enough for them to allow Tony Peña to go into free agency (he eventually signed with the Red Sox).

The club's strong fight for the division title was witnessed by a new St. Louis attendance record of 3,082,000.

August A. Busch, Jr.

Busch Stadium, St. Louis, with the city's famous arch in the background.

"I think our staying in the race as long as we did is what helped him go on a little longer at the end." This is what Whitey Herzog said upon learning of the death on September 29, 1989, of August A. Busch, Jr. The owner of the Cardinals, described in one obituary as "the master showman and irrepressible salesman who turned a small family operation into the world's largest brewing company," was ninety years old and had been in failing health.

"Gussie," as he was familiarly known to the public at large, was celebrated in the world of commerce as the genius behind the growth of Anheuser-Busch to a sales point of nearly $10 billion a year. But it was as the owner of one of baseball's proudest franchises that he became best known to the public. From the time he

bought the team in 1953 for $7.8 million, he had sought success and savored it when it came. August Busch riding into his stadium before league playoff or World Series games in a wagon drawn by an eight-horse hitch of Clydesdales, waving a red cowboy hat to the cheers of the crowd, had become part of the legend of St. Louis baseball.

No team in the National League has been more successful than the St. Louis Cardinals. Throughout the league's long history, none of its member clubs has put on the field more players of front-rank splendor, of record-making propensity.

As the century enters its final decade, Cardinal fans can look back with pride and satisfaction, and ahead with anticipation. Unlike many fields of endeavor, the time spent by baseball is not for baling and stacking; it is, rather, an ever-modifying mosaic of memories, of recollections of crisply hit balls, of wondrously thrown pitches, of balls excitingly and artfully caught, of men on the dash around the stations of that flawless geometry known as a baseball diamond. Every fan has access to this magical elixir of remembering, this sweet call to youth and American summer. For St. Louis Cardinal fans it has always seemed like a little more, for theirs is a team which has continually extended its own style of eye-catching baseball. And through it all—the headfirst slides, the acrobatic catches, the uproarious times—those two redbirds on the front of those St. Louis uniforms have remained poised and steadfast, as though always absolutely confident of victory.

APPENDIX

CARDINAL LEAGUE LEADERS

HOME RUNS

1922	Hornsby	42	1936	Medwick	64	
1925	Hornsby	39	1937	Medwick	56	
1928	Bottomley	31	1938	Medwick	47	
1934	Collins	35	1939	Slaughter	52	
1937	Medwick	31	1941	Mize	39	
1939	Mize	28	1942	Marion	38	
1940	Mize	43	1943	Musial	48	
			1944	Musial	51	
			1946	Musial	50	

TRIPLES

1915	Long	25	1948	Musial	46
1917	Hornsby	17	1949	Musial	41
1921	Hornsby	18	1950	Schoendienst	43
1928	Bottomley	20	1952	Musial	42
1934	Medwick	18	1953	Musial	53
1938	Mize	16	1954	Musial	41
1942	Slaughter	17	1963	Groat	43
1943	Musial	20	1968	Brock	46
1946	Musial	20	1979	Hernandez	48
1948	Musial	18			
1949	Musial	13			
	Slaughter	13			
1951	Musial	12			
1966	McCarver	13			
1968	Brock	14			
1977	Templeton	18			
1978	Templeton	13			
1979	Templeton	19			
1985	McGee	18			

RUNS BATTED IN

1920	Hornsby	94
1921	Hornsby	126
1922	Hornsby	152
1925	Hornsby	143
1926	Bottomley	120
1928	Bottomley	136
1936	Medwick	138
1937	Medwick	154
1938	Medwick	122
1940	Mize	137
1946	Slaughter	130
1948	Musial	131
1956	Musial	109
1964	Boyer	119
1967	Cepeda	111
1971	Torre	137

HITS

1901	Burkett	228
1920	Hornsby	218
1921	Hornsby	235
1922	Hornsby	250
1924	Hornsby	227
1925	Bottomley	227
1936	Medwick	223
1937	Medwick	237
1942	Slaughter	188
1943	Musial	220
1944	Musial	197
1946	Musial	228
1948	Musial	230
1949	Musial	207
1952	Musial	194
1964	Flood	211
1971	Torre	230
1979	Templeton	211
1985	McGee	216

DOUBLES

1911	Konetchy	38
1920	Hornsby	44
1921	Hornsby	44
1922	Hornsby	46
1924	Hornsby	43
1925	Bottomley	44
1926	Bottomley	40
1931	Adams	46

BATTING

1901	Burkett	.382
1920	Hornsby	.370
1921	Hornsby	.397
1922	Hornsby	.401
1923	Hornsby	.384
1924	Hornsby	.424
1925	Hornsby	.403
1931	Hafey	.349
1937	Medwick	.374
1939	Mize	.349
1943	Musial	.357
1946	Musial	.365
1948	Musial	.376
1950	Musial	.346
1951	Musial	.355
1952	Musial	.336
1957	Musial	.351
1971	Torre	.363
1979	Hernandez	.344
1985	McGee	.353

WINS

1926	Rhem	20
1931	Hallahan	19
1934	Dean	30
1935	Dean	28
1942	Cooper	22
1943	Cooper	21
1945	Barrett	23
1946	Pollett	21
1960	Broglio	21
1970	Gibson	23
1984	Andujar	20

STRIKEOUTS

1930	Hallahan	177
1931	Hallahan	159
1932	Dean	191
1933	Dean	199
1934	Dean	195
1935	Dean	182
1948	Brecheen	149
1958	Jones	225
1968	Gibson	268

EARNED RUN AVERAGE

1914	Doak	1.72
1921	Doak	2.58
1942	Cooper	1.77
1943	Pollet	1.75
1946	Pollet	2.10
1948	Brecheen	2.24
1968	Gibson	1.12
1976	Denny	2.52
1988	Magrane	2.18

INDEX

Southworth, Billy
  manager, 59, 97
  move to Boston, 116
  statistics for, 1926, 47
  trade from Giants, 44–45
  World Series, 1926, 48
Spink, Al, 2
Spring, Jack, 168
Staley, Gerry
  statistics for
    1949, 136
    1951, 138
Stanky, Eddie, 138–139
Stock, Milt, statistics for, 1921, 37
Street, "Gabby" Charles, manager, 61
Stuart, Johnny, 40
Stupor, John, World Series, 1982, 210
Sudhoff, Willie
  move to Browns, 9
  statistics for, 1901, 9
Sutter, Bruce
  move to Atlanta, 212
  statistics for
    1981, 206
    1982, 208
    1984, 212
  trade from Cubs, 205
  World Series, 1982, 209, 211
Swisher, Steve, 204
Sykes, Bob, 206–207

Tatum, Ken, 190
Taylor, Jack, 12
Taylor, Ron, World Series, 1964, 172
Teachout, Bud, 69
Team records
  1930, 61–62
  1939, 94
  1943, 107
  1944, 110–111
  1948, 133
  1949, 136
  1952, 142
  1953, 143
  1954, 145
  1957, 153
  1968, 182
  1975, 194
  1982, 208
  1983, 211, 212
  1985, 215, 216
  1987, 224
Tebeau, Patsy, 4
Templeton, Garry
  statistics for
    1976, 195
    1977, 197
    1978, 199
    1979, 201
    1980, 203
  trade to San Diego, 207

Tenace, Gene, 204
Thevenow, Tommy
  injuries, 55
  World Series, 1926, 48
Thompson, Milt, statistics for, 1989, 231
Torre, Joe, 185
  MVP, 1971, 189
  statistics for
    1970, 187
    1971, 188–189
    1973, 190
Toth, Paul, 168
Triple Crown winner, Medwick, Joe, 86
Trolley Car World Series, 111
Tudor, John, 217
  injuries, 223, 227
  playoffs, 1987, 224
  statistics for
    1985, 216
    1986, 223
    1987, 224
  trade from Pittsburgh, 215
  trade to Dodgers, 228
  World Series
    1985, 219, 220
    1987, 225, 226

Uecker, Bob, 172–173
Union Association, 3
Uribe, Jose, 215
Urrea, John, 204

Van Slyke, Andy, 212
  statistics for, 1985, 215
  trade to Pittsburgh, 223
Verban, Emil, World Series, 1944, 113
Virdon, Bill, Rookie of the Year, 149
Von Der Ahe, Chris, 2
  manager, 3
Vuckovich, Pete, 205

Walker, Bill, statistics for, 1934, 74
Walker, Harry, 95, 107
  manager, 149
  trade to Philadelphia, 130
Wallace, Bobby, 4
  move to Browns, 9
  statistics for, 1901, 9
Waller, Ty, 205
Warneke, Lon
  Gashouse Gang caper, 85
  statistics for
    1939, 94
    1940, 95
    1941, 98
Washburn, Ray, 177
  statistics for, 1968, 182
  World Series, 1968, 183, 184

Watkins, Bill, 3
Watkins, George, statistics for, 1930, 61
Weiland, Bob, 85
Western League, 6
Westlake, Wally, 138
White, Bill, 157
  doubleheader hitting record, 160
  statistics for
    1962, 162
    1963, 165–166
  trade to Philadelphia, 172
White, Ernie, 95
  statistics for, 1941, 98
  World Series, 1942, 105
Wilks, Ted, statistics for, 1949, 136
Willis, Ron, 177
Wilson, Hack, 69
Wilson, Jimmie
  All-Star Game, 73, 1934
  statistics for, 1930, 61
  trade of, 57
Wilson, Owen, statistics for, 1914, 25
Wise, Rick, 190
  statistics for, 1971, 189
World Series
  1926, 47–50
  1928, 57
  1930, 66
  1931, 67, 69
  1934, 75–76, 79
  1942, 104–105
  1943, 107
  1944, 111–113
  1946, 123, 125–128
  1964, 169, 171–172
  1967, 177–180
  1968, 183–184
  1982, 208–211
  1985, 219–220, 222
  1987, 225–226
World War II, effect on Cardinals, 106, 109, 115
Worrell, Todd, 217
  injuries, 234
  playoffs, 1987, 224
  Rookie of the Year, 223
  statistics for
    1987, 224
    1988, 228
  World Series
    1985, 220, 222
    1987, 226

Young, Cy, 4, 5
  switch to American League, 9
Yuhas, Eddie, statistics for, 1952, 142

Zeile, Todd, 234